## PRAISE FOR ERIN & BRIDGES TO HEAL US

Part memoir, part a call to action, Erin Jones' debut is engaging every step of the way. Her stories of the past connect us to the steps needed in the present to move into equity for all built around our common humanity. As a sixty-eight-year-old white woman learning more about race and relationships every day, I read it to learn how to put beliefs into words and actions. After reading the book (which I will revisit often), I'm more hopeful and inspired to keep listening and working for equity for all with renewed commitment.

—Karen Burns, Retired librarian

Erin Jones is the voice we need now more than ever. She draws us in as only a gifted teacher can, presents the truth as we need to know it, and inspires us to write a new story of relating and healing that must happen to save lives and our soul as a nation.

—Grace Leaf, Spokane Community Colleges

The author provides a glimpse into her life—her stories are powerful and her practical strategies lay a foundation for US as we pursue racial equity and justice. After reading *Bridges to Heal US: Stories and Strategies for Racial Healing*, I am committed to bringing my "best and bravest self" to this work as we "link arms and build bridges together." Let that be US.

—Cari Harrison, Dean of Students
Bellarmine Preparatory School

The stories told in *Bridges to Heal US* make learning about a topic as vast and often daunting as racial equity a less scary journey. Erin's ability to open herself up to others and use her experiences to inspire others to make change creates a deeper understanding of what she is teaching and why, and creates a safe space and community for people to begin their work in the world of social justice. This book is a call to action above all else, but it also provides ample evidence as to why a call to action is needed and what can be done to create change.

-Kath Shelden, 10th Grader/Sophomore

"Bridges to Heal US" is a poignant reflection on the significance of race in America, chronicling years of Erin Jones' experience as an educator, politician, and her unique perspective as a foreign-raised Black woman in America. Through this work, Erin uses her lived experiences as a tool for creating connections, inspiring empathy, and sparking change.

-Diya Anoop, 12th Grade (Class of 2022)

# BRIDGES TO HEAL US

## STORIES AND STRATEGIES FOR RACIAL HEALING

Michael,
Thank you for
your service!

E.J.

STORIES AND STRATEGIES FOR RACIAL HEALING

# BRIDGES
# TO HEAL
# US

## ERIN JONES

Editing: Andrae D. Smith Jr.

Cover Design: Emily's World Of Design

# DEDICATION

I dedicate this book first to the people who chose me in the beginning, my parents. Without them, this book, my life as it is, would not be possible. I love you so much, Mom and Dad! You show me every day what unconditional love is, and because of you, I can love so many others unconditionally.

I dedicate this book to my husband, James, my biggest champion, second only to my parents. Thank you, Honey, for your patience and forgiveness, and constant support. Thank you for treating me as an equal partner on this journey.

I dedicate this book to my children—to those I birthed out of my body, Malachi and Israel, our adopted daughter, Reneeka, and to my older, White, chosen child-now-man, Joshua. I am proud of each one of you for what you have done, but even more importantly, who you are becoming.

I dedicate this book to Jenni, my daughter-sister, Malachi's first babysitter, who cared not only for him but for us, at a time in our lives when we had nothing and could hardly see a way forward.

I dedicate this to the thousands of students who have been in my classrooms (physical and virtual)—the young and the old—who have also been my teachers. A special shout out to Anna and Lucy and Damaris and Jake, who just keep showing up!

I dedicate this to the virtual community that joined me during the pandemic, who believed in me when I had no idea how I would make ends meet, when I felt powerless to make the kinds of change I knew needed to happen to heal this nation.

I dedicate this to the Equity Institute—to Fernell, Dr. Jen, Vincent, Dr. Mollie, Paul, Bonita, Roy, Michelle, Joe, and Sebrena, all the others who continue to show up week after week.

I dedicate this to #therootofouryouth and #becoming (you know who you are).

# EPIGRAPH

"Sisterhood"

I want to be the me I didn't have as a girl.
I want you to love your hair and your skin and your curves and your height (or lack thereof).
I want you to know you are smart enough and pretty enough and strong enough.
I want you to know it's ok to not fit in (because the girls who say they do are really just pretending).

I want to be the me I didn't have as a young adult.
I want you to know you don't need a man.
I want you to know you don't have to know where you will be 20 years from now.
I want you to know mistakes are part of the journey.

I want to be the me I didn't have as an executive.
I want you to know your voice matters.
I want you to know you belong there.
I want you to embrace opportunities to learn from other great women.

I want to be the me I didn't have as a politician.
I want you to know you can be your full self, even if they say it will lose you your election,
I want you to be the author of your own story.
I want you to maintain your integrity, because you'll have to live with yourself afterwards, win or lose.

I want to be the me I didn't have, so you can be the you you're meant to be.

BROOKE BROWN, WA STATE TEACHER OF
THE YEAR 2020

Covid-19 has shifted the realities for so many of us. During closure last spring, I read an article that helped name what we were all going through—grief. This is a season of grief and gratitude. We need both to make it through. This summer felt like everything we had relied on has shifted. There is a divide in this country that seems insurmountable. The pandemic, the west coast on fire, the murder of George Floyd, everything seemed to be spiraling out of control. The world felt like it was upside down.

To add to all the uncertainty, I was pregnant in the pandemic, delivering our beautiful son on a late Thursday night in July. He let out a loud cry, and behind a mask, I shed tears of joy. He was healthy. Beautiful. Just what we never knew we were missing. Born at thirty-six weeks, he was a little premature but spent no time in the NICU. We would find out later on that he has an extra chromosome—Trisomy 21. I didn't know what to do. I was lost. The grief was consuming. I realized, over time, that there was joy. We just have to keep looking for it. Searching for it.

The many people in our community lifted us up. People that I had poured into were now pouring into me. People delivered dinners and dropped off gifts, but the most important thing they gave us was their presence. They showed up to show me, to show us that they cared.

They sat with me, socially distanced, and listened. They advocated and researched and were there. Sometimes no words were exchanged. There were phone calls, video chats, text messages. People shared space. Their presence was the best present. My son brings so much joy to our lives and the lives of those around us. He has the best smile, sleeps through the night, and gives the best snuggles.

I have learned that through difficult things, when our circumstances are outside of our control, we must shift our perspective. We cannot shrink and step back. We must make space for grief and acknowledge its presence so we can continue to show up. We must dry our tears and get back to life. Community and connection are what we need to get through this pandemic and through life. We need one another.

As I pen these pages, I am full of grief *and* gratitude, joy *and* sorrow. So much of life is about living in the space of "and." Our state recently reopened, and though restaurants are full, and many folx feel like they can return to "normal," I am reminded of something I heard Sonya Renee Taylor say that became the foundation to help me endure these past 16 months. She said, "We will not go back to normal. Normal never was. Our pre-corona existence was not normal other than we normalized greed, inequity, exhaustion, depletion, extraction, disconnection, rage, hoarding, hate, and lack. We should not long to return, my friend. We are being given the opportunity to stitch a new garment. One that fits all of humanity and nature."

How are we working to stitch a new garment instead of longing to return to the before times? We have all lost so much, in the next few days, I will attend services for two amazing women who I have had the great privilege to learn from. One is my maternal grandmother who transitioned a few weeks ago. She was born in Rhode Island, married a complicated man, and gave birth to 9 children in

11 years. She was the glue that held that family together—always had a witty comeback, loved fiercely, and was wildly inappropriate as she gold older. She was beautiful and loving in all the best ways.

My grandmother in love, (my husbands grandmother) was born and raised in Georgia had 3 beautiful daughters and never had the chance to go to school. That didn't stop her from sharing her wisdom with all of us every week at Sunday dinner. Her dishes were the best because of the secret ingredient she always included, LOVE. We would sit around the table and listen to her tell us stories about growing up, and she always started cooking the day before so she could go to church and then come home and finish. I am a better person because these beautiful women have loved me.

Being bi-racial, I have always felt on the outside, like I didn't quite fit in. My role in the social change ecosystem has always been a bridge builder, helping people see each other's perspectives. I met Erin when I was in middle school, and she has helped shape me into the woman I am today, the wife, mother, friend, sister *and* the 2020 Washington State Teacher of the Year. She has been my mentor and friend and has consistently reminded me of who I am and challenges me to use my voice to be brave.

I read a story from Humans of New York today, where they interviewed Big Mike, and he said either you are serving your community, or you are taking. How can we continue to serve one another? How can we love one another? It's not hard—we put one foot in front of another and keep loving—ourselves, our families, our co-workers, and our neighbors. We keep having those hard conversations and keep leveraging our humanity. Erin introduced me to Christian Paige—with whom I had the opportunity to record a podcast—and he reminded us that "we will never best practice our way into real relationships." We have to keep showing up, keep being brave and keep loving one another.

Thank you for picking up this book. I look forward to the impact you will have on those around you.

# PREFACE

This book was birthed out of fifty years I have spent living as a Brown woman born out of the body of a White woman.

This book was birthed out of a childhood witnessing nations in conflict try to seek peace and healing through the International Court of Justice in The Hague, The Netherlands.

This book was birthed out of four years of torment in college, trying to figure out how and if I belonged in the United States.

This book was birthed after thirty years of professional life watching systems harm students, not because people sought to harm but because we avoided having honest conversations about race.

This book was birthed in response to the most contentious political season I have witnessed in my fifty years of life that illuminated in new ways our need as a nation to face the truths of our history and learn to talk to and walk with one another.

I write this book not as one who claims to know all the things necessary to get us to racial healing and wholeness, but I offer what I do have: hope, stories, and strategies.

# I SEE YOU

I see you!
     I have watched you closely since 1989, when I returned to the United States for college, after spending my childhood at the American School of The Hague in The Netherlands. I have borne witness to the subtle and more explicit cues you gave me that in America, one should never speak of three things in mixed company —race, politics, religion.

I experienced your silence throughout college, as I tried to navigate race in America for the first time, as someone told me that I had only earned my spot in this elite space because I had brown skin. I experienced your silence when I was followed in the pharmacy as I looked for toothpaste, not because I had done anything wrong but because my skin sent a message that I was a thief; meanwhile, you moved about the space without a second thought. I experienced your silence when I was seated at the back of the restaurant, alone in a corner by the door, as you and your friends sat with all of the other patrons towards the front, with the light of the windows, not the stench of the garbage cans. I watched you squirm in your seat, on occasion, wanting to do something but unsure what to say.

Then there was a glimmer of something in 1991 when local and national news outlets played footage of the beating of Rodney King by LAPD officers after a high-speed chase during his arrest for drunk driving. Then, for the first time since my arrival in the United States, I heard you talk with classmates about the intersection of race and justice. However, you still had not made the connection to the ways race played a role in how Black and Brown students experienced school differently than you had or who had access to home loans or who would get the lead role in a play on Broadway or a film out of Hollywood.

The killing of Trayvon Martin awakened you. I listened to your conversations in teachers' lounges and checkout lines at the store. Together we watched as large groups of people marched in protest in major cities and on college campuses across the country. Suddenly, you seemed aware that maybe skin color did change how people could move through the streets of this nation.

While working for the State Superintendent, I saw numerous efforts to "eliminate achievement gaps" and ensure educators were "culturally competent." My former Black and Brown students spoke of being recruited right out of college to fill new quotas in this business or at that government agency. These moves affected some of you but still did not translate to significant, sustainable action. I watched you attend trainings and conferences where you continued to see the "usual suspects." The very people who most needed to be in the room *never* seemed to get there. Maybe some of you were starting to see that, too.

Then there was the murder of a child, Tamar Rice, in 2014. And then Walter Scott in 2015 and Philando Castile in 2016. I saw you pay attention beyond the bare minimum required at work. I saw you begin to understand the difference between equality and equity and form connections to education and healthcare and housing and justice.

I watched you try to navigate intense conversations about what it would require to serve Black and Brown students better. When our state passed a law requiring schools to incorporate the histories of our Native tribes into the curriculum, I watched you embrace that new learning and make every effort to get your colleagues to do the same.

When I ran for statewide office in Washington State, I watched you engage in new ways as I shared my campaign platform in front of you in legislative district meetings and regional political debates. I could tell you knew you should be caring about equity but were not exactly sure how in the context of your local schools or how that should translate into legislation. No one running for State Superintendent had ever talked about racial equity before. Even though you had heard stories of Black and Brown students experiencing school spaces differently, you had not considered how school systems were targeting Black, Native, and Latinx students. You had not considered the ways other systems—like housing, health care, and policing—impacted students differently. You watched as even my opponents began speaking of these issues in ways no one had before.

I saw another shift in you in 2016, as the United States experienced the most contentious Presidential election in my lifetime.

I watched you engage in the political process in new ways in reaction to eight years with our first Black President. I saw two groups of people emerge in response to President Obama: (1) Those who thought we had arrived at racial harmony, as evidenced by his election, and (2) those who were so disgusted by his having been President that they were determined to vote Republican in the next election, no matter who the candidate was.

Many of you who thought we were post-racial, as evidenced by the election of a Black man to the highest office in the country, did not have close Black friends and assumed that the Obama election was evidence racism was a thing of the past. You assumed his election was a sign that America was a place where truly anyone could accomplish their dreams if only they worked hard enough. You assumed we had done enough work in years past to produce greater racial harmony. You were shocked by those around you who expressed elation and "good riddance" at the end of Obama's second term. Those who spoke of him and his family with distaste, who never said his color had anything to do with their disgust but who did not seem to value his commitment to his wife or the proof he gave that he was Christian, not Muslim. You were shocked at the continued accusations of President Obama having not been born in the United States, no matter the evidence to the contrary. Why so much hate, you wondered?

I watched as you tried to navigate the pervasive "us" vs. "them" dynamics that seemed to take place on every social media platform during the 2016 political season on topics from pro-life vs. pro-choice to what to do about immigration and how to improve access to schools. I saw you bear witness and even participate, on occasion, in mudslinging and dehumanization, which seemed to become the norm for that election cycle.

I saw you respond to the results of the election with shock, then grief, and then anger. For a time, you went silent, as if the wind had been taken out of your sails.

You and I witnessed four years of US—from the top of government to the neighbor a few houses down—denigrating anyone not in "our group." I experienced US deteriorating in our ability to talk to anyone outside of our "clan" about anything of substance.

Then the pandemic hit, and I watched you try to navigate both the health and social epidemics as the news of Ahmaud Arbery, Breonna Taylor, and George Floyd unfolded on your television screens and in your social media feeds.

I watched you change your profile picture to show your support for #BlackLivesMatter, and then you posted about the need for everyone to read How to Be an Antiracist by Dr. Ibram X. Kendi. I saw you post about the podcasts you were listening to and the things you were learning.

I have watched you attempt to navigate this complicated season by just "liking" posts at first, worried about saying the wrong thing. Then, I watched you make an effort to step out and engage with others.

Some friends and family you thought you knew well hunkered down with "their people" and embraced their belief systems more strongly than ever. Other members of your circle avoided any conversation about race or politics and sent you private messages asking you to stop posting so much about all this "race stuff."

Like me, I watched you navigate church spaces that were being more and more divided along political and social lines. You and I struggled as we saw those who had seemed gentle and meek now take strong stances in ways that felt contentious and dehumanizing, who suggested that the mere mention of race was, in itself, "racist."

Instead of running FROM those conversations, I watched you seize the opportunity to run INTO them, wherever people were open, even in the slightest. I watched you try to provide support to friends in interracial marriages and friends with transracially adopted children who were trying to navigate already complicated conversations about race and justice. I watched you struggle with what to say, feeling helpless at times to find the right words.

If you are asking the question, "What can I do to be part of racial healing and justice in the United States of America," this book is for you.

If stories inspire you, you will find them here.

If you need strategies to help you move forward in your learning, you will also find those.

I want to close this chapter with a short story about why we must engage on issues related to race, and why now is the right time for US to have these meaningful conversations. I recently gave a presentation to the staff of a credit union. I shared pieces of my story, the very ones you will see in future chapters. As usual, most of the audience members were White people, who had very different experiences from my own. I had to trust that my message would resonate with at least some of them.

In the last of a three-part series for the credit union, a staff members shared what they had learned over the previous trainings. One of the managers shared about how one of my stories had helped her as she tried to support one of the members of her staff. One day a Black man entered her branch to access services. This branch was a different one than he normally frequented. When the teller asked for two forms of identification, the man became very upset. He never had to present two forms of ID at his branch. The teller explained that it was their policy at this branch to ask for two forms of ID. The gentleman became incensed. Another staff person called the manager to ask for her support out front.

The manager came out, ready to defend her staff person, but as she approached the man and listened to his concerns, she was reminded of a story she had heard in my presentation—a story of my having been profiled in a store. She suddenly understood why the man was so upset. He was being treated differently from the way he was used to being treated and felt he had been racially profiled. It felt to him as though he had been singled out. The teller did her job to explain the policy but missed the real reason the man was upset. When the manager arrived, she understood his story. She explained to the man what she thought had happened and was sure to apologize for how it appeared, and she was able to help him and the teller through an uncomfortable situation.

As you read this book, you will get to know more about me and how I have used my story to understand people and then help them listen to the stories of others around them. I hope to show you a way to better serve those around you with very different stories and experiences.

I hope this book will provide you at least the beginnings of an answer to your questions. I am writing this book to each of you who is questioning your role in the racial healing of our nation.

Wherever you are in your journey of discovery regarding racial healing and justice, I am sure you will get a lot out of this book. That said, I am writing specifically to that person who has already done some reading, attended at least a training or two on diversity and equity, and knows they need to understand and DO more.

# 2

# HOW I CAME TO CARE

My journey into conversations about race and equity, ignorance and knowledge, brokenness and healing began fifty years ago when I was born brown out of the body of a White woman in a hospital in Saint Paul, Minnesota.

My biological mother did not keep the little brown baby she had carried in her womb for nine months. I started life at the Children's Home Society. A White couple from Northern Minnesota, who had never met Black people, decided to adopt Black babies, and at three months old, I became part of the very Scandinavian Adamson family.

My parents had grown up in the tiny Iron Range communities of Coleraine and Grand Rapids. Although Grand Rapids is now one of the largest towns in the area, it is no metropolis. Outside of the Chippewa people, who typically live on or near the Reservation, you can probably still count the number of people of color on both hands who live in that region today.

My parents had no idea the challenges their decision to adopt Black babies would bring them—both within their families and in the community in which they chose to make our home in Central Minnesota.

I still remember my first conversation about race as a child. I was attending the birthday party of another preschool-aged child, and she asked me why my skin was always dirty, "Doesn't your mother ever give you a bath?"

I had not considered until that moment why my brother and I were the only brown people in our neighborhood. Maybe we really were dirty. Maybe my mother had the wrong soap, which is why we were the only brown people. I remember making a bee-line for the bathroom, where I tried to scrub the brown off my skin.

My father came home from work weeks later and announced to the family that he had taken a job teaching in The Netherlands. Considering neither my mother nor my father's families were travelers, it still amazes me my parents decided to fly across the country and then across an ocean to give my brother and me a very different life experience than they had as children.

My parents had no idea what they were getting into with the move. My father just knew he wanted to teach overseas somewhere, and he took the first job offered to him—teaching middle school math at The American School of The Hague. The school served American and international students whose parents worked for embassies, the State Department, or the global oil industry. Because my parents taught at the school, my brother and I would attend (a very expensive school) free of tuition.

I went from being orphaned in the Twin Cities to being adopted by two small-town Scandinavian-Americans to then sitting in classrooms with very powerful people's children. Every American President who came to visit the International Court of Justice would walk the halls of our small private school, from Jimmy Carter to George Bush.

Although I had traveled to multiple countries and was already fluent in two languages by nine years old, it was fourth grade that set the stage for my work today. That year my best friend was the Israeli ambassador's daughter. Israel and Palestine were in heavy conflict in the late 70s and early 80s, and suicide bombings and shootings regularly made the front page of the newspaper. Imagine life before the internet, when all you knew was what the newspaper printed once a day. My friend had family in Israel and never knew who was impacted by the previous day or week's events. I was drawn to her story and to the Israeli people.

One night my parents dragged me to a PTA meeting, and who was sitting at the main table in the library but my friend's father, the Israeli ambassador. Across the table from him sat the ambassador for the Palestinian Liberation Organization. It turned out his child also attended our school.

Israel and Palestine were in the same building... at the same table!

The nations were at war, and here were the fathers, sitting across the table from one another, talking about their children's education. If they could talk in such civil ways about education, I had a notion I could convince them to talk about peace between their nations.

I was nine years old.

I was so inspired by the idea of facilitating peace between these two nations that I began to learn to speak Arabic and Hebrew. Instinctively, even at nine years old, I knew I had to be able to speak both of their languages if I was going to build a bridge between them.

As fate would have it, that same year, the nation of Egypt found itself embroiled in a civil war. The President's wife, Mrs. Sadat, had a particular passion for young people and a desire for peace. She had the idea to deliver school assemblies to elementary school children on the subject of peace. She believed if small children could commit to peace, over time, wars would cease. She decided to do a trial run of her presentation idea in our small American school. In late winter of 1981, Mrs. Sadat showed up at our school with her personal friend, John Denver, who sang several songs with our school choir (all I remember now is "Leaving on a Jet Plane"), and then she shared her message.

When the presentation was over, I was one of three fourth-grade students invited to eat with Mrs. Sadat and John Denver. She asked us to introduce ourselves and then share how we hoped to change the world. I was so eager to go first. "Mrs. Sadat, I have decided to solve the Middle East Crisis. I want to bring peace between the Palestinians and the Israelis. I am learning to speak both Arabic and Hebrew."

She looked me right in the eyes, "Erin, you are a world-changer!"

She did not say, "Someday you will be a world-changer." She did not tell me I had a lot of potential. She told me I was, right at that moment, a world-changer.

I was determined from that moment on to live my life the way a world-changer would. I invested 100% in every activity—from schoolwork to athletics to music. My friend from Israel left my school the following year, so I no longer had a Hebrew tutor, but I would pick up French and Spanish. I knew I had to speak many languages if I would do the world-changing work I knew I was called to do.

When I arrived in high school, there was no doubt I needed to prepare for college. Almost 80% of the students in my school, regardless of their familial origins, came to the United States for college. I was expected to do the same. I took all the most challenging classes (eleven Advanced Placement courses included), played two instruments in the band (earned a spot in the international honors band, even), played three varsity sports (all of which I captained and earned MVP awards), and served as the President of the Security Council for the largest Model United Nations in the world.

My first acceptance letter came in March of 1989. I had applied for early acceptance at Princeton. College letters did not come to our homes in those days. The guidance counselor received all our acceptance and rejection letters. That day a surprise announcement was made over the loudspeakers just before lunch, "Erin Adamson has been accepted at Princeton University."

I was over the moon! All the AP classes and extracurriculars had paid off! I was going to my first choice institution. My dream was to go to Princeton for undergrad and then to Harvard Law School. I planned to return to The Netherlands with a law degree and work as a lawyer at the International Court of Justice.

When I returned home that night, Mom and Dad sat in weighty silence at the dining room table. "Erin, we are so proud of you, but... it looks like Princeton must not have considered our financial aid paperwork because your financial aid package is only $1000 per year. We are so sorry. We saved money for your college education, but not enough to pay tuition at Princeton."

I do not know who was more devastated in that moment—my parents, who had watched me work so hard over a lifetime, or me.

Two weeks later, the other letters started pouring in from small liberal arts colleges. Several offered significant financial aid packages. One offered a full scholarship. Finally, I received notification from my second choice, Bryn Mawr College, one of the elite Seven Sisters colleges. I knew this is where I needed to attend. The package was significant, and Mom and Dad said they could afford tuition there.

Although I was still disappointed I would not be attending Princeton, Bryn Mawr was a great institution with high status. I could still earn an undergraduate degree in pre-law and get to Harvard, and Bryn Mawr was located in a city with which I had fallen in love through watching the Cosby Show. I loved the Claire Huxtable character. She was the kind of woman I hoped to be someday. She was classy and witty and brilliant and accomplished and a great mother. We watched the show every Thursday evening from my sophomore year to graduation. I imagined myself attending college in the neighborhood of Philadelphia, where the show was set. I was excited by that prospect.

Unfortunately, because my parents were teachers, we did not have the money to visit Bryn Mawr. However, I felt, after seeing the pictures in the brochure and watching the Cosby Show, I had a pretty good idea about what the environment must be like. In August of 1989, I boarded a plane with my mother, and we prepared to fly from Schipol Airport in Amsterdam to Philadelphia International Airport. Mom planned to stay in town near the college for a week to help me get acclimated (as if one can get acclimated to an entirely new culture/country in a week).

We did not arrive in the United States until midnight. Every restaurant in the airport was closed. Mom and I arrived at baggage claim only to discover my luggage had been lost, "Ma'am, give us a call in two weeks, and we will let you know if we have located your bag."

Two weeks? I was hungry and had *nothing* to my name to start my new life in America. This was flying pre-internet. All they could do was guess where my luggage had been sent.

Mom and I hopped in a taxicab, one of the last ones in the airport that night. She was asleep within minutes. Although I was tired and hungry, I was also so excited to start a new season of my life in "Cosby Land!" I was wide-eyed as we left the grounds of the airport and hit the freeway. The cab driver drove and drove and drove. We were no longer in the city of Philadelphia. The houses kept getting bigger and bigger. Finally, we passed a sign that said "Bryn Mawr." We were getting close. Just a couple blocks later, on the main road, was another sign, "Lower Merion Cricket Club, no coloreds or Jews allowed here."

What?! Had I seen the sign correctly?

I swiveled my head back to read the other side of the sign. The same message was there, front and back, just off the main road, not a mile from the college campus, "No coloreds or Jews allowed here."

I had studied American history, probably more thoroughly than most children raised in the United States. I had taken Advanced Placement US History, but my parents also had intentionally bought me books about the history of Black people in America, so I knew about Slavery and Reconstruction, Jim Crow, and the Civil Rights Movement. This was not what I expected in "Cosby Land."

I was suddenly more afraid than I had ever been until that moment, and I had a decision to make. Should I wake Mom up?

I made a choice that night, in a split second, to not tell my mother about the sign, to pretend as if it had not been there. She would not learn of its existence until I was in my late 30s, and she heard me tell my story on a public stage for the first time.

That sign was a great predictor of the kind of college experience I would have. On day one, when I entered the cafeteria for breakfast and tried to speak to the only other Black people there, who happened to work as dining hall staff, I was pulled aside by the head cook, who informed me that, although we were both Black, students and dining hall staff were not, ever, to interact with one another. "Honey, you are obviously not from here, but you and us...we are not the same. You should not be talking to us."

That made no sense to me at all.

I had come to campus a week early for soccer pre-season. Other first-year students began to show up midweek for orientation activities. That first Wednesday, I was scheduled to attend a course selection event. Mom came with me. I remember standing in line waiting to complete paperwork with her beside me. When we arrived at the table and were asked to complete a document, I was first stumped by a social security number request. Although I had been born in the United States, I had never used that number before. Fortunately, Mom was able to produce the actual card from her wallet. She was prepared.

What happened next changed us forever.

"Choose *one* race—White, Black, Asian Hispanic."

The document was clear. I could only choose *one* race. I remember staring at that portion of the form, unsure which bubble to color with my pencil. This was another designation I had never had to consider in all my years attending the American School of The Hague. I mean, I knew I was both Black and White, based on my adoption papers and appearance, but I had never had to identify as such in writing.

I stared blankly at the piece of paper, unsure how to proceed. If I chose "Black," would my mother feel like I was denying her and my father? But I could not choose "White." No one would believe I was only White. Tears began to well up in my eyes.

Although I had said nothing to my mother, she could feel my confusion, pain, and concern. She could see where I was on the paper.

I can still remember the words my mother whispered in my ear, "Just put 'Black,' honey. It's ok."

I love my mother. I am sure she hugged me. She is and has always been my biggest champion.

The end of the week came. Mom returned to The Netherlands, thousands of miles away. In 1989, there were no cell phones. There was no internet. There was no email.

We could send phone calls through the school operator, but those calls cost five dollars a minute. My parents had enough money to pay my tuition, room, and board, but they did not have much extra to give me. So I would have to get a job just to be able to call home once a week.

I had no idea what loneliness could feel like until my mother was gone.

In week two, as I headed to class one morning, a White student approached me. Without any malice in her voice, just matter-of-factly, she stated, "You know you are only here because we have to have ten of you."

Huh?

"Excuse me? Ten of who?"

"Black women. We have to have ten Black women each year to

get money from the federal government. It's called 'affirmative action.'"

And she walked away, just like that.

I made the mistake of walking across the street to the Admissions Office to get clarification. What was this woman talking about? I had never heard of this thing called 'affirmative action.' How could I be here because of my skin color? I did not even know what it meant to "be Black" at that point.

The poor Director of Admissions had to explain to me what Affirmative Action was and confirm that, yes, I was one of the ten Black women in my class.

I thought I had earned admission at Bryn Mawr with my 3.9 GPA, eleven AP classes, four languages fluent, three varsity sports that I captained, and had been selected MVP for two years running. I suddenly wondered, 'Had I really earned my spot here?'

Doubt began to creep in for the first time.

The following week, I headed to the pharmacy to buy a new tube of toothpaste. As I left campus and prepared to cross the main street into our tiny downtown, two young men drove by me in a Jeep with the top down, its tail plastered with Villanova University stickers. "Get out of our neighborhood, Ni—r!"

I felt like I had been punched in the gut. I had read that word in books before, but I had never heard the word out loud and *never* directed towards me. I literally could not proceed to the store. I suddenly felt unsafe. I turned around and ran back to my dorm, curled up in my bed, and cried myself to sleep.

That would not be the last time racial slurs were yelled at me.

Fall turned to winter, and I joined the varsity basketball team. So many upper class women had knee surgery that year. I became one of the starters and played every single minute of every game. We won every game that year for the first time in many years at the college. As much as I loved playing, it was a challenging experience socially as the lone freshman starter. I was respected as a player, but I did not drink at all, like the other players, so I spent most of my time alone when we were not at practice or on the road.

When basketball season ended in March, I no longer had any community. No one checked on me to see how I was doing. I stopped going to class. I stopped eating. I stopped taking showers and washing my clothes. I know now, I was depressed. I did not fit in anywhere. I was too European for the few Black women on campus. I had been raised internationally, but I was an American citizen, so I did not qualify for international student support. White people had raised me, but I also was not White.

On the first Saturday of April 1990, I woke up to a brilliant, sunny day and knew I needed to get off-campus. I did not have a car, and I did not have money to catch the train into town, so I threw on shorts, a t-shirt, and tennis shoes and began to walk. I had no idea where I was going. I just knew I needed to get away. After an hour of walking, I happened into a community with significantly smaller homes than the mansions of Bryn Mawr. Everyone in the neighborhood looked like me. Everyone was Black. For the first time, no one stared at me. It was like I belonged there.

I could hear basketballs bouncing in the distance. Several blocks ahead of me was an outdoor basketball court. A game of streetball was about to start. "Hey, girl! We need one more to play five-on-five! Get out here!" A very tall man yelled toward me. "Come on, girl! You are obviously a baller!"

I mean, he was not wrong. I was a basketball player. I got out and played with this group of men—a blend of those in their late forties and young ones in their mid-to-late teens, all Black. The tall man who had called out to me was one of the oldest on the court, but he was also clearly the best. I would learn his name later—the one and only Dr. Julius Erving (the creator of the slam dunk).

We played all afternoon. Eventually, Dr. J. took his young adult sons home, and I sat on the sidelines with three young men about my age. "Where are you from?" one of them asked. "You ain't from around here. You talk funny."

"I am from The Netherlands."

"The Nether-what?"

"You know... next to Germany."

"Germantown (a town just outside Philadelphia)?"

"No. Germany, in Europe."

"Where's that?" another boy asked.

"Wow! Where do you go to school that you haven't learned where Europe is?"

The three boys had all stopped going to school years ago. They described schools in North Philadelphia that were falling apart, where there were not enough books or even chairs for all the students.

"Wait! I thought children *had* to go to school in America...."

"No one ever noticed we were gone," one of them said.

"So, what's your dream for the future if you are not going to get a high school diploma?" I knew there were not very many options in the United States for people without diplomas.

"Dreams?" They began to laugh. Or maybe they were crying. "We don't expect to live to twenty-one. Why would we dream about a future?"

I felt like a freight train had hit me. Here I was, having spent the last several weeks in bed, depressed, wanting to just disappear from the earth, not believing I fit in anywhere, thinking maybe there was no way I could change the world. Suddenly, I knew, all at once, I had been born brown out of the body of a White woman, abandoned and adopted by White people, who chose to raise me at one of the best private schools in the world for this! I knew exactly how I was meant to change the world.

I ran back to campus, tears streaming down my face the entire way. I got to my dorm and called the operator, "Can you please put me through to my parents in The Netherlands?"

When my mother answered the phone, I burst into tears, "Mom, I love you and Dad so much! Thank you for being my champions, and thank you for choosing to change the world every day as teachers. I never saw you as world-changers before, but now I do. Now I get it!"

Each of our stories is different.

We each have a different role to play in the healing of our land. You may have grown up in an all-White home and community. You may not have traveled beyond the boundaries of your zip code. You may still spend most of your time with people you have known since you were a small child. Your story still matters in our healing.

Part of our problem at the moment is that we are each running in our own race without sharing the stories of our triumphs and struggles. This leads us to believe we are running against one another instead of on the same team.

You can change the world, too, by sharing your story and listening to the stories of others. In sharing stories, we are exposed to our humanity—the reality that each of us has won and lost in life; each of us has experienced heartache and failure at some moment. Each of us has gifts that could be used to benefit both our families and those we do not yet know. So often, our continued segregation—often merely circumstantial—in housing, schooling, and places of worship creates distance, suspicion, and fear.

I knew at nineteen years old that I had no choice but to use the unique story I had been given, the pain I had experienced, the rejection to build bridges to help others. I did not know exactly where this realization would lead me long-term, but I knew it meant significant change.

Mom and I cried as I revealed my newfound realization of how much she and my father had done for me. However, I had an even more important message. "Mom, I know now how I want to change the world. I know what I was made for. I know I have said a million times I never wanted to be a teacher like you guys, but now I know that's exactly what I am meant to do. I am supposed to teach right here in America. I am supposed to be a champion for kids who look like me. They deserve to get what I got, to have people believe in them as you believed in me." I paused. "Mom, I know I can't come home."

We cried some more.

Now you may be wondering what happened next, and I promise I will tell you, but I want to take a moment to explain why I have shared all of this. As you can see, I did not grow up with the "typical" Black experience. I had to learn it. I knew the history but had not lived it. As I gained experience with life in America, it became clear what I am here to do. And that is where this book comes in. So what makes me qualified to write to you? Why should you pick up this book and trust Erin Jones will give you something valuable?

I do not claim expertise on the subject of racial equity. I do not have advanced degrees on the topic. I have not been personally trained by Dr. Ibram X Kendi or Dr. Beverly Tatum. I have read their books, as well as books by Dr. Brenda Salter-MacNeil, Jemar Tisby, and Dr. Martin Luther King, Jr.

Most of what you will read is based on almost fifty years of living as a biracial, Black-presenting, Afro-wearing, born-in-the-United-States-but-raised-in-Europe-by-White-adoptive-parents, Bryn Mawr College graduate, wife to Black man, mother to three Black young adult children, thirty-year veteran K-12 educator, and Jesus girl.

After so many years, I am an expert in my own experiences, and I believe my experiences can help others think and behave differently. I have lived in two countries and visited twelve others. I am a fairly fluent speaker of three languages besides English. I have been involved in church ministry in all-Black churches, multi-ethnic churches, and predominantly White churches. I have taught in various urban spaces, from 100% Black North Philadelphia to South Bend, Indiana to Columbus, Ohio, to both the West and East sides of the state of Washington. I have raised two biological children with my Black husband (yes, his race matters), and we adopted his niece at nine years old, so I have also raised a Black girl into adulthood.

I have experienced the difference between being treated as an American, in a time in the 1980s when Europeans valued American presence (for the most part), and being treated as a Black woman in America, when I returned to the United States for college in a time when there were still signs identifying which establishments were not welcoming to Black patrons.

I am an expert in the norms and values of middle-class White people because that was my environment during my formative years. It is the experience of my parents, their families, and most of my childhood friends. Middle-class White values and ways of doing work, business, and school have also been the norm for most of the work environments I have found myself in over the last thirty years.

That being said, my marriage to a Black American man raised in an urban setting by a single mother showed me entirely different ways of being. Our experiences living in all-Black or predominantly Black communities in both South Bend, Indiana, and Columbus, Ohio, taught me that what I had come to believe was "normal" was not at all; what I had experienced in all these spaces was just *one* way of being. Learning to survive and thrive in those communities and in my own marriage required years of self-reflection, reading, and learning from experts.

Teaching and volunteering in various communities taught me to embrace not just one way of learning and being. I learned to recognize and affirm the many ways people experience the world and make their way through it, sometimes with success, other times having to overcome incredible barriers. These opportunities also taught me that systems and structures have been set up to serve some well and to hinder the flourishing of others. I also learned over time that oppression does not require the actions of evil people. Spaces where only some flourish can occur merely by the silence of those being served well.

I cannot be silent.

Once you know better, you must do better. I have not yet arrived at my final destination in this work. I will continue to learn right alongside you. I hope that as you take this journey with me, your curiosity will be piqued, and you will commit fully to self-reflection, new connections, and a willingness to take the actions necessary for your own healing and for the healing of all of US who call the United States home.

I have spent the last thirty years of my professional life working in and around schools. I have used my expertise in language and culture to help both students and educators see the diversity of colors and cultures and languages other than English as assets. I have now worked in state government and school district administration with a focus on racial equity. In addition, I have run for public office to lead schools in Washington State with a focus on racial equity and justice.

Concurrently, I have spent thirty years serving and leading alongside my husband in the Black Baptist Church and then predominantly White charismatic churches. We have lived in a 100% Black community, where we had our first son and where we were the only family not "from" the community. As a family of four and then five and then six (my husband's mother, who integrated Franklin Pierce High School in the late 50s, lived with us for six years), lived in communities where every home represented a different ethnic background. We have lived in communities where we were the only family of color, where our children became not only the only Black children but the only children of color in their schools.

I have witnessed the harm that is caused when we do not talk about race. I have watched the division created when those who are experiencing harm try to talk about that harm with others and experience disbelief, absolute silence, or even anger ("how dare you suggest..."). I have also watched so many make new connections, develop new funds of knowledge and skills and step into becoming bridge-builders devoted to racial healing.

I do not claim to have arrived. I am still on my own journey of self-discovery and healing. I am still adding tools to my tool kit as I meet new people with different experiences and skill sets.

The work of racial equity and reconciliation is not easy, but I believe I was physically made and given the life story to *be* and to *build* bridges to heal US. I am committed to living my destiny. May we link arms and build bridges together.

## 3
## WHAT TO EXPECT

I closed the last chapter crying with my mom on the phone after explaining that I would not be able to return home. The truth is, I returned home for vacations on occasion. Still, I never did live in The Netherlands again. I met my husband at a college summer program for Black students in Boston in 1991. We were married two years later in South Bend, Indiana, where he was completing his master's degree in American Government at the University of Notre Dame and where I got my first teaching job.

After my husband completed his master's, we left South Bend. We moved to Columbus, Ohio, where he attended Bible college for almost a year before being called to his home church in Tacoma, Washington. He became the youth pastor and the first Black person on the church's all-White staff.

We made the conscious choice when we moved to Tacoma that I would not teach right away. We had two little boys, and I knew what happened to little Black boys who entered school without being able to read, write, and do math. So we made a choice to live on his pastor's salary. I stayed home with the children. During those early years, we took in another child. My husband's sister struggled to make good life decisions, so her daughter came to live with us. We quickly had three children, one year apart. (The two youngest are born the same day, a year apart).

When the children were still pre-school age, I was invited to try out for the WNBA for both the Seattle Storm and the Portland Fire. I became the oldest woman with the most children at WNBA tryouts. I made NBA LIVE at my second tryout for that feat (LOL— I guess there are worse things to make the news for). More importantly, I was seen by a former Olympian, a woman who had played on the very first US Women's Olympic basketball team, who happened to be at tryouts in Portland.

I realized by the second tryout that, as much as I loved basketball and was better than average, I was not good enough, nor was I in my prime. However, this coach was impressed by my work ethic, attitude, and leadership skills. She watched me from a corner all day. When the event was over, she approached me to ask if I would consider being the player-captain of the American practice squad she was arranging to play against the Mexican Olympic team the next summer. For many reasons, I could not join her that summer, but on my thirtieth birthday, June 3, 2001, I played against the Mexican Olympic team in our first exhibition game. We played games in different outdoor stadiums in Mexico City over the course of several weeks that summer.

When I returned to the United States, I received a call from my cousin on my father's side. All of us on that side are six feet tall or taller. All of us are basketball players and educators. All of us have coached high school basketball. My cousin called me to ask if I would be willing to fly to Northern Minnesota to coach a girls basketball camp with him.

"Only if you arrange for me to meet with Grandma when I get there."

My mother and her stepmother had not spoken to one another (that I knew of) since I was nine years old, the year she married my grandfather. We were invited to Christmas in Minnesota that year. Of all eight grandchildren, my brother and I were the only two children of color. We were also the only two not to receive Christmas gifts. That experience sent a clear message to my mother about what her stepmother thought of us. Each time we returned to the United States for vacation, we only saw my father's parents. We no longer visited with my mother's. Although my grandparents showed up at my wedding in 1993, we did not see them before or afterward. I wanted to understand what had caused the fissure.

To make a long story short, I would visit my (step)grandmother after the first day of camp. She met me at the door of her apartment in the retirement home. In her hands, she held a shoebox filled with every school picture and certificate and newspaper clipping from my childhood into my young adult years. It turned out my mother had been sending these things to her father all this time.

"Erin, do you know we were more proud of you than any of the other eighteen grandchildren? We just didn't know how to tell you because you are a ni—er."

Yep. She said THE word, the word you should never say.

"Grandma! You can't say that word!"

"What am I supposed to call you, then?"

It was at that moment I realized my grandmother was not a horrible human, as I had at times suspected. She was just incredibly naive and ignorant. How could a hateful person both believe I was amazing and call me a horrible name?

"Grandma, how about you call me Erin?"

"Erin, I am so sorry. Can you ever forgive us? Your grandfather went to his grave and never got to tell you how much he loved you."

We both began to cry. I held all 4'11" of her in my arms for what felt like an hour.

At that moment, I knew I had been made and raised to engage in racial reconciliation work. It was apparent that if so much division could happen in my family because we avoided any conversation about race—if our family could be almost destroyed due to our lack of honesty—it was no wonder our nation was so divided along racial lines.

I finished out the weekend of camp and headed home, knowing that, as much as I loved teaching middle school students, I needed to make sure I also did everything in my power to be and build bridges to heal our brokenness as a nation around race.

My (step)grandmother died within the next few months.

What if I had not tried out for the WNBA?

What if I had not gone to Mexico for the summer to play against the Mexican National team?

Would I have ever had that moment with my (step)grand-mother? Would we have had that opportunity to bond and heal? That is what I want to do with this book. I want to create opportunities for all of us to come together to end the division that is destroying US.

This book is a series of stories and strategies designed to help US develop the skills and knowledge necessary to both BE and BUILD the bridges we need for our healing as a nation around issues of race and justice.

Although I am a trainer in racial equity, I am first a storyteller.

I am not sure how this happened. I was the crazy tall, shy kid in middle school and then in high school. Although my parents are both *amazing* educators, I would not describe them as storytellers. We read immense numbers of books growing up, and I can remember my parents reading me stories at bedtime as a little girl. They were not tellers of their own stories at home or in their class-rooms. (I had them both as teachers in high school, so I have studied their pedagogical styles in context.)

I think my extensive experience in Black Baptist churches as a college student—watching Black preachers weave stories through their sermons every Sunday and during Bible study during the week —may have introduced this style. I grew up watching very polished presenters read sermons from a pulpit. In West Philadelphia (in the same neighborhood in which Will Smith was raised), I watched pastors who knew the Bible well but also knew they needed to connect their Bible knowledge to the personal lives of their congregants. I watched preachers who understood the power of tempo and volume, the importance of humor and passion. I witnessed sermons that reminded me of performances I had seen on stages and on film screens. Similar styles were reinforced in the classrooms in which I volunteered in North Philadelphia during my last two years of college, where teachers were masterful in verbally engaging students. Teachers knew how to connect in authentic ways with their students. They knew they could not merely share information, that they had to connect heads to hearts in ways that would compel students to pay attention.

I have always been a student of people in different spaces. As someone who had to navigate many cultures and various spaces as a young person, I had to be "studious" of my surroundings for my survival. Over the years, I watched what engaged people. I watched the ways stories were connected. I watched the ways whole groups of people were humanized when their unique stories were told.

This book is a blend of stories and strategies for you to employ as you seek to do the work of bridging gaps, of being and building bridges in your communities, classrooms, business offices, places of worship.

I hope that as you hear my stories, as I share vulnerably about the good, the bad, and the ugly in my life as a daughter, a mother, an educator, a politician, and a community member, you will reflect on your own stories and the ways you can use your stories as bridges to others and as learning opportunities. I hope my stories will inspire and challenge you to become a better version of yourself, engage in different ways in your professional spaces, and work locally and nationally for racial justice.

This book was birthed in response to many people over the years asking me to tell my story and in response to those who have attended my racial equity training and want more. I hope the blend of story and strategy will help you move your learning forward and help you engage others in this journey because it will take *all* of US to move the US in the direction of healing and wholeness.

I have done training on topics related to race and culture since I took on a role at the State Superintendent's Office in 2008. However, I have been doing racial equity training almost exclusively as a consultant since January of 2017, just weeks after losing a political race to lead public schools in the state of Washington. I had not intended to become a trainer in racial equity. After losing my election, when people asked what my plan was, I had to inform them, "I didn't have a plan. I don't play to lose. I play to win."

Starting in January of 2017, organizations and school districts began to reach out with requests—for keynote addresses, assemblies, and trainings. By January of 2020, I had developed a rhythm in my work. Typically, the first week or so of the year was devoted to helping staff and students return to business with short keynotes and assemblies, where I would rally the troops, help teachers remember their WHY, and help students get re-acclimated to the school setting and set goals for the upcoming semester. Mid-January was the parade of Martin Luther King, Jr assemblies. Typically, I speak at anywhere from twenty to thirty events, depending on the year. February brought a blend of equity trainings for schools and businesses, as well as a flurry of Black History Month speeches across the state.

For the first time ever, I was invited to be the keynote speaker at the Indiana State college admissions conference in Indianapolis near the end of February. I was extremely excited about this opportunity, not only because it was one of the biggest venues to which I had been invited, but also because I had been married and had taught in the state of Indiana, just a few hours north of Indianapolis, in South Bend. I flew out several days early and visited my son's first babysitter, a math teacher at a local high school. She arranged for me to do an assembly at her school. Then I had the opportunity to visit the private school I had taught at for a couple of years (where Pete Buttigieg was an 8th grader at the time). I was even able to visit with a student from my very first class. She was working in a school nearby as a tutor, but during a lunch break, I got to visit her in her first home and walk the community where she now lived, where she was invested, as I had been twenty-seven years earlier.

Who could have known this would be the last time I would get on a plane for over a year? Who would have guessed, then, that the crazy schedule that had me flying and driving and speaking, often in eight to nine cities per week, was about to grind to a halt in a matter of days after my return home?

It was the week of March 9. We had begun to hear stories of this strange ailment that had overtaken an elder care facility and stolen the lives of many just north of Seattle, just over an hour north of where we live. There was suspicion that this infection had been brought to the care facility by someone who had visited after a trip overseas. There were news stories on a daily basis about how quickly the virus was spreading, concern that it was airborne, and worry about how to contain it. Organizations hosting large conferences were beginning to send out notifications of possible cancellations, but no one knew at the time the level to which we needed to be concerned.

My assistant received the first cancellation that week. I was disappointed I would not be flying to Washington, DC, to speak at my first national conference. I was just scheduled to do a workshop, but I was still disappointed. I love visiting DC.

By Wednesday, March 11, everything had been scrubbed from my calendar. I mean, there was nothing left on my calendar at all. This was of grave concern for me because I am not on salary anywhere. No events means no paycheck. When I jumped into consulting, I knew I was taking a risk, but I had become fairly successful. I was now bringing in more money than my National Board-Certified Teacher husband. Suddenly, I had nothing to bring to the table.

I did not say anything to my husband right away because I was terrified. He is the bill-payer in our house. I was so afraid that losing my income would put us behind on our house and car payments. I knew how my husband stressed when bills were over-due. We have lived that life—the one where we lived in the red and ate just bean and rice—before. It was not fun. I was not trying to go back there, but I did not know what to do. I did not know how I could bring in money without schools and conferences.

On the evening of March 12, I rolled over in bed and shared the news with my husband as we were getting ready to go to sleep.

"Honey, you are always doing. Don't worry about it. We are going to be fine. Why don't you just BE for a while? We won't be able to go out to eat or go to the movies for a while, but we will be fine."

I could feel my body collapse in relief. Little did I know our state was about to be shut down. We were not going to be able to go out to eat or go to the movies or to the Mall anytime soon, anyway.

Just be? How to do that...

March 13 is a day I will remember for a long time because our Governor had already made the announcement that schools would be closed. Although we did not yet know much about the virus, we knew it was highly contagious. He had already warned people not to be around those who were older or who had pre-existing health issues. My parents fit into both of those categories. My mother's mother had died of complications related to pneumonia when I was nine years old, and my mother tended to have a bout of pneumonia annually. My father was dealing with kidney issues. March 13 is my mother's birthday, and I knew I could not see her. Well, I could see her, but I could not get close. I knew I should not go into her house, and I could not hug her on her birthday.

I brought my mother's gift over to her home, left it on the front steps, called her to let her know it was there, and then went back down the stairs to wait for her to open the door. At forty-eight years old, I cried as I sang Happy Birthday to my mother from the street, terrified in the moment that maybe this would be her last birthday with me. We had no idea at the moment how severe this virus was, and I was suddenly very aware of my parents' mortality and my own.

By Saturday morning, I had an idea. I remember going to bed Friday night with this thought in my head—"Erin, what do you have in your hands? What is a talent you have that you could give away in this moment?"

I was no longer worried about making money, but I felt compelled to put something out into the universe that would be a gift to others. As I considered that question, I knew that I had an iPad, and I had 20,000 or so followers on social media. I also knew that I had a love for teaching.

As I watched my social media feed just from Thursday to Saturday, I witnessed parents who were now worried about what they were going to do with their children. Thursday afternoon, at a press conference, the Governor and the State Superintendent made a joint statement canceling all schools for the next two months. Parents who were still unsure about their work schedules were trying to figure out how they would navigate this shift in responsibility. I watched teachers try to figure out what they were supposed to do. Were they going to be required to teach from home somehow? What was that going to look like? I watched the older students I was connected to stressing out about AP exams and already missing their friends.

I knew exactly how I needed to respond.

On Monday, March 16, I began to go LIVE on Facebook each weekday morning with a read-aloud in English Monday and Wednesday, Spanish Tuesday and Thursday, and French or Dutch on Friday. Stores were still open for a bit, so I rushed to Half-Price Books, purchased every decent children's book I could find, and created a small library. I decided to offer an online racial equity course, also via Facebook LIVE, for any educators who were interested in adding some tools to their toolkits. I went LIVE over the lunch hour each day with a "Becoming a Change Agent" course for students from elementary through high school.

Although I already had twenty to thirty hours of material on racial equity developed from my time at the State Superintendent's Office and then from my time as the Director of Equity for two different school districts, I had to rethink how I delivered this material on Facebook in one-hour chunks without being able to see any of my attendees. I only had the chat feature to receive any feedback or respond to any questions.

At the end of the first week, a college student reached out to me, "Erin, it's so awesome that you are teaching on Facebook right now, but I think it's hard for people to really engage on Facebook. Why don't you use Zoom? We use it in our classes for college. It allows everyone to see everyone else."

Zoom? What the heck was that? I had no idea what "a Zoom" was or how to "get one."

I began to do research. Fortunately, Zoom had seen into the future and knew their service was going to be of incredible value to many, so getting an account was free for a year. I got an account and began on that platform the following Monday. I would open a Zoom room and set up my iPhone to continue to go LIVE on Facebook for anyone who continued to want to join that way.

What began with just a few educators I had known for years in Federal Way and in Tacoma became a "classroom" full of paraeducators and classroom teachers and instructional coaches and administrators from across the state of Washington and, on occasion, from other parts of the country. By the end of the second week, I could see the need to incorporate additional material into my curriculum because educators asked specific questions and wanted to go deeper. Suddenly, what had been just a couple dozen hours of material had now become days and weeks of content.

Of course, what I could not have predicted was the murder of Ahmaud Arbery and then Breonna Taylor in the midst of all of this. And then there was George Floyd at the end of May. So much death. So much grief. So many examples of why this work was so critical.

We were already scared as a nation. We were seeing more Black and Brown people get COVID 19 and die because of it or lose their jobs because they had to miss work as they healed or because they had no one to watch their children.

Now, suddenly, we were witnessing Black death, filmed and uploaded on every social media platform, being aired on repeat from every news station. Ahmaud Arbery was particularly poignant because I am a runner and run through "strange" neighborhoods all the time while I am on the road as a speaker. In addition, my son was the same age. I made the conscious choice not to watch any of the footage of the murder. Life was already scary enough without subjecting myself to the brutal murder of another young Black man. Breonna Taylor lay sleeping in her own bed when she was killed. What could she have done differently?

I was already sensitive after Ahmaud and Breonna. When George Floyd's death hit the news, I was devastated. Not to mention, I was born in St. Paul, Minnesota (the city that borders Minneapolis). I found myself in deep sorrow, trying to make meaning of this violence that was taking place all around us, this apparent targeting of Black bodies.

Fortunately, I had created this community of practitioners, now friends, who walked with me through this difficult season, who lamented with me. There were classes where all I could do was cry. Another teacher would take over facilitating for the day, so I could just be present. On other occasions, I would wake up to a knock at the door. Someone from class had driven from wherever they lived —sometimes from over an hour away—to leave a card and hot coffee or a bouquet of flowers outside my door.

I do not know that I have ever experienced such great care from a community of people.

Who is in your community as you do this work?

You cannot do this work on your own. You will need a community to learn alongside you, to lament with you as you read a story or as you suddenly realize ways you have caused harm to people on your job or even in your family. Who can you enlist to join you in this process?

After the murder of George Floyd, a friend posted a Tweet with a link to something called "The 21-Day Racial Equity Challenge" and tagged me, suggesting "someone" should facilitate this process for folks. I assumed he was tagging me because he was suggesting I should host a group. I was not feeling like doing any more training at that moment. I was tired of training. I did not feel like my little trainings were doing anything to move the needle on this problem that felt overwhelming.

After letting the Tweet sit for half a day, I suddenly had an idea: What if I offered to facilitate a group of just White leaders in The Challenge?

Leaders had influence and could change systems. I did not have the energy for the average person who may or may not take this information and do something useful with it. I felt an urgency to help leaders get this equity thing right, finally. People had been talking all around equity and completely avoiding conversations about race. This avoidance is what got us here in the first place.

My first class would start just two weeks later. A White friend who was only connected to me via social media sent me a private message, "Hey! I am trained to deliver racial equity training. If you ever decide to deliver training, I would love to partner with you, and I want to do it for free. I feel like the best way I can support a Black woman is to invest in this way."

Dr. Jen Self and I delivered that first training, which has now been followed by numerous other opportunities.

Businesses and schools, and government agencies began to reach out for training. Now that open racism had been displayed on repeat for all of the world to see, leaders knew they had to, finally, engage in meaningful ways. Who could help them in this work but the woman who had been going LIVE on the topic every day on social media?

This book is a by-product of the several trainings and coachings I have developed for leaders across various professions. What you are about to read is much like my training—a blend of story and strategy. I hope after fifteen chapters, you will feel prepared to share and use your stories in new ways, to be and build bridges within and between your spheres of influence. I hope that you will learn from my pain and the pain of others to show up in new, more effective, more compassionate ways that lead US (the United States) to healing.

In the upcoming chapters, you will be introduced to some of the most important terminology related to equity. You will learn the differences between work as it relates to diversity, culturally responsive practice, and equity. You will learn the distinctions between the terms "race," "ethnicity," and "culture." You will become comfortable with the language of racial equity. I have learned that so many of our miscommunications and lack of unity is connected to a lack of common language, so we will begin by covering that. You will then walk through the three phases I take schools and businesses through—unpacking your own story, considering the ways people of different identities may be experiencing the world differently from you, and then interrogating the larger systems at play in this nation. You will make practical connections to the role you can play in interrupting systems in your workplace, in your community, and at state and federal levels. Finally, you will be given ideas for how to help others join you on this journey and recommendations for how you can continue to grow in your knowledge and practice of equity moving forward, especially when you come up against barriers and obstacles.

Let the journey begin!

4

# SETTING THE STAGE

Much of the work of racial equity, of being and building bridges, is developing and practicing new postures and attitudes towards the work. So many of the skills and coping mechanisms I have created, I learned through sports, both in organized settings and on my own as a hobby.

I started playing soccer at five years old and then added baseball (which transitioned to softball) and then basketball. I played organized sports four to five days a week until I was forty-five years old when running for statewide office made it impossible to continue getting up four mornings per week at 4 AM to play pick-up. Either the hubby or the hobby was going to have to go. Eliminating the hobby was easy, especially as I watched so many of my friends in their forties and fifties tear Achilles tendons or severely sprain ankles. I made the conscious choice to go out on top, with no significant damaged body parts.

Because I have been an athlete my entire life, my body needs movement. I made the decision to do as many walking meetings as possible during the campaign. I did all of my fundraising calls while walking Tacoma Mall. I walked either in the mall (when it was raining) or in whatever neighborhood I found myself between meetings. During the year of my campaign, I walked an average of five miles per day.

When I lost my election, one of my best friends, who raised top athletes and knew I had been an athlete most of my life, knew I needed something immediately to work toward. She knew I needed to set a goal for which I had complete control, which was unlike running for office (no matter how hard you work, success is not in your hands but the hands of the public). My friend recognized that, although I had worked with incredible effort, under the most difficult of circumstances, and only lost by less than 1%, I probably struggled with feeling like a failure.

"Erin, I think we should run a half-marathon."

Run? Long-distance? Me?

I mean, I had been running with a ball for decades, but the idea of running just to run made no sense, especially long-distance. I loved wind-sprints during practice. I was fast. The goal was very clear. That being said, she was correct. After losing such a close election after so much hard work and overcoming so many obstacles, I needed a win—one over which I had complete control of the outcome.

I began to train. I started with just one mile of running and then a mile of walking, and then another mile of running. I worked my way to running three miles at a time. After a month of running three uninterrupted miles four to five times per week, I pushed myself up to four miles and then challenged myself to run on the treadmill for one hour straight.

Two weeks before the race, I ran the seven-mile trail along Ruston Way in Tacoma, Washington, on two different occasions, non-stop. I never did get up to the entire 13.1 miles of a half-marathon, but I suspected once I got into a rhythm, I would be able to go the whole way without stopping for rest.

In June of 2017, I ran my first half-marathon with my friends Marina and Jill. I ran the entire 13.1 miles without stopping one time. I continue to challenge myself to run different races, usually once a quarter. Knowing these races are coming forces me to keep training, to continue to stretch myself.

Preparing to talk about race effectively is kind of like preparing to run a long-distance race. You cannot jump in and expect to go deep in your first conversation, just like there is no way a first-time runner could complete a 10K or a half-marathon without any training. In fact, your first conversation about race is likely going to be really uncomfortable, just like running the first mile in training.

If you want to be successful in this endeavor, you will need to commit to a long-term plan. Part of that plan will require not only training yourself but learning how to respond to those who will inevitably say this work is not necessary or this work is not for you.

I believe the work of talking about race and justice is for everyone, of every color and every background. This work is for you, whoever you are. This work is for me. The work is for US; it is necessary for our healing.

For those who would suggest that conversations about race create division, I would argue that our division already exists. Much of our division is caused by our lack of skill and comfort with talking about hard things. Having grown up in another country, one of the things I have found to be truly "American" is that there are three things Americans are encouraged not to discuss in mixed company—race, politics, and religion. Talking about these topics with those who do not hold the same beliefs creates incredible discomfort. As a nation, we have prioritized temporary comfort over having the honest conversations required to move US to our healing. Our unwillingness to talk about hard things has amplified a lack of skill, more than anything. Our division is exacerbated by a culture of shame, blame, and guilt that leads to defensiveness and, therefore, an inability to fully engage in the important conversations required to move US forward.

So much of having conversations about race, justice, and healing is about the attitudes, behaviors, and demeanors that are necessary to do this work effectively in a way that produces long-term change and flourishing. This chapter will not address the content of racial equity work in depth but the approaches I have come to believe are necessary to even begin the work, the emotional and mental containers to hold the work so it is sustainable and effective.

I believe my years teaching in the nation's poorest Title I middle school classrooms prepared me well for the work of talking about racial equity. Not only did I come to understand the ways we resource and educate the nation's poor and Brown children differently than White children. I also witnessed how we often describe and define success based on ideas and principles that do not align with Black, Brown, and Native communities' notions of success. Not to mention, these communities' ways of being are very different from the ones with which I came to be associated in my home and school.

I felt called to serve in schools where the student body looked more like me than the school where I grew up. However, this reality meant I needed to learn different ways of being. I needed to learn to meet my students and their families where they were, not to insist that they come to me on my terms (an attitude I adopt even as I write this book for you now).

Those first years of teaching taught me quickly the importance of being intentional in the opening days and weeks of class. I had to set the tone by creating a culture that invited students to step into their best selves—to take risks, embrace a willingness to fall and fail and get back up, and learn to trust me and each other. I spent most of my career in school spaces where authority was not easily trusted, where being "the teacher" was not a guarantee of respect, where students had learned to be suspicious of adults and, even, of their peers.

Fifteen years of classroom teaching and coaching experience prepared me to work with adults as a facilitator and trainer. To be honest, we adults are just big twelve- and thirteen-year-olds. We are easily defensive and disappointed, and hard on ourselves. We are anxious *to* try new things and do all we can to avoid discomfort (more than the average middle school student, in fact).

For this reason, the beginning of every training is spent creating the environment necessary for hard conversations, which I believe is critical to success. For the last year, since the first week of school closures in March of 2020, I have made a practice of starting every event—every keynote, every facilitation, every training—with gratitude. Four educator friends and I co-wrote a book called "Thrive" that was published in February of 2020. My friend, Dr. Jenny Severson, wrote a chapter in the book about her doctoral work on the subject of gratitude. I learned from her research that gratitude is not something some people naturally demonstrate more than others. Gratitude is something that has to be practiced, developed like a muscle. In fact, the more gratitude is practiced, the more "normal" gratitude becomes. Regular practice even changes one's brain chemistry.

I began to practice gratitude with intention every day early in quarantine. I lost a friend to a heart attack in February of 2020, and then I lost my first friend to COVID 19 in March, just as we were learning about the virus. I would go on to lose five more people over the next three months—four to a variety of cancers and one on the operating table during a routine tumor removal surgery. I believe the practice of gratitude helped me keep my head above water and focus on what remained good and hopeful in my life.

If gratitude was an essential strategy for me, I thought it would probably also be helpful for others. So I started asking participants in each of the Zoom rooms I found myself in to share their gratitude in the chat as a way to start each session. I found that starting with gratitude set a positive opening tone for the difficult conversations that were about to happen.

What are you grateful for in your own life right now—big or small? How can you make gratitude a part of your daily practice? For example, could you keep a gratitude journal? Could you encourage every family member to share their appreciation at dinner each night? Could you open staff meetings with gratitude where you work?

Once we practice gratitude, I introduce the idea of "brave spaces." Many over the last decade, especially on college campuses, have talked about ensuring "safe spaces" for students of color, especially when there were controversial speakers on campus. My children, who were all recent college students, always thought the notion of "safe spaces" odd. They never felt completely safe on their campuses at any point in time.

I do not believe there is a way to create spaces that are "safe" for everyone to talk about hard things. In fact, after doing this work for so many years, I do not believe safety should even be a goal for which we strive. Thinking back to my days in the classroom, I do not think I would describe the climate of my classroom as "safe." I did want students to be comfortable, but, more than comfortable, I wanted students to be brave, to be willing to try hard things and fail and get back up. I did my best to model those things myself.

Too often, in staff meetings, we are "safe." We create spaces with "meeting norms" that discourage honest conversations, vulnerability, and authenticity. As a linguist (fluent in English; semi-fluent in Dutch, French, and Spanish), I believe words are important. "Norms" is short for "normal." I was raised by middle-class White people in a middle-class White school and a middle-class White community. I attended a middle-to-upper-middle-class, predominantly White college. I am an expert in the "norms" and ways of doing business that are common to White spaces. What has become expected as "normal" in most work and school spaces looks exactly like what was "normal" for my experience in my home and in the education spaces where I learned and taught, "don't rock the boat," "don't speak unless you are spoken to," "don't challenge those in authority," "don't show your emotions," "don't speak until your answer is perfect." None of these ways of being create the kind of environment necessary for hard conversations. Furthermore, to suggest, especially when talking about race, that the prescribed "safe" norms, values, and ways of being of middle-class White people should be centered is highly problematic.

The reality is that those who are not "safe" in most education spaces and professional environments are typically the very people who live mostly in the margins—women, people of color, and those who identify as LGBTQIA+. The "safety" of White people is typically prioritized in predominantly White spaces, so the necessary conversations never happen. I cannot tell you how many of my friends and colleagues have been accused of creating a hostile environment simply for trying to raise a concern about how they or how their students of color were being treated. When I served as an administrator at both the state and in the district office, I was often the only or one of the only Black women present. I was often informed that I needed to stop raising issues of race (even when there were others who raised issues related to socioeconomic background and special education far more often). I was told that my mentioning race made people feel uncomfortable, which meant we never learned to address these critical issues, leaving educators unprepared to address the needs of their students and the students' families.

Not talking about a thing does not make it go away. Not talking about a thing does not create an environment of "safety." I would suggest that pressure to be silent about controversial issues is a significant sign that the environment is not "safe."

Through high school and into my young adulthood, I assumed the way I had been raised and the way things ran in my school were "the way." Even in my first year of volunteering in an all-Black school in North Philadelphia, my attitude towards students who called out to the teacher without raising their hands or who talked loudly in the hallways or who danced around their desks during lessons was that they were behaving "badly," instead of realizing that their "norms" and ways of being were just different. I learned this by watching another teacher, Sheila Drapievski, embrace her students and meet them where they were. She helped me realize there were different ways for students to show they were engaged. She also helped me to understand and value success in different ways. She created spaces that allowed her students to show up as their full selves, which informed the kind of environments I create for my students and for adults to do the difficult work of moving toward racial equity.

Sheila allowed students to call out their answers without raising their hands, just like they would do during the sermon in their local Black Baptist Church. She allowed students to sing as they worked or to make rhythms on the tabletop, as they did in their neighborhoods when they were not at school. Instead of demanding her students remain perfectly still, she recognized their need to move and took them outside for a brief game on the sidewalk in front of the school when they became fidgety. Most importantly, she did not demand that they become like her. She met them where they were and invited each one to become the best version of themselves.

"Erin, not every Black child wants to become a middle-class White person, and why should they want to?"

I am now married to a Black man, who I met after my sophomore year of college. He was raised as a latch-key kid by a single mother in an urban center. He and his brother both attended large state universities on full-ride football scholarships. Both also have very successful professional careers—my husband as a high school teacher and head football coach and his brother as one of our state's most renowned investigative reporters. Even though we have all experienced academic and professional success, our cultural norms and ways of moving through the world are very different. My husband's family thinks about time differently than mine. They engage openly in conflict. They demonstrate passion openly—joy, frustration, anger. They are loud... always.

My husband and I have been together now for almost 30 years. Being with him has taught me that there are not "right ways" to be. I have had to learn that I embody ways of being that are actually helpful to him and ways his family operates that are much more healthy. There is not one set of cultural values that are pure or right. However, in the United States, there are messages—both explicit and subtle—that communicate to everyone that White middle-class values are the only acceptable ones. In a nation as diverse as the US, with a history as complicated as ours, we must be willing to pull from the best of US all.

Every culture has its pros and cons, its assets and deficits. If we are going to create the kinds of spaces that encourage everyone to engage in difficult conversations that are necessary to move US (the United States) towards healing, it will require courage and bravery, not safety. If we are honest, the people we tend to worry most about being "safe" in these conversations are White people. Let us set the tone for everyone to step into the ring with the same expectation for bravery and courage.

I invite all of my training participants into a space that encourages them to be their "best and bravest" selves. Here are some recommendations of community agreements I offer at the beginning of every class:

• Embrace a posture of learning, not fixing

• Take risks—the more vulnerable you are willing to be, the more you will get out of this experience

• Push through the inevitable discomfort that will come; do not let it paralyze you

• Show grace to yourself when you make mistakes and towards others when they do

• Apologize when you make a mistake ("I am sorry" is not always easy, but it costs you nothing)

• Realize that there is more than one way to experience this country/community—just because you have not seen it or experienced it does not mean "it" has not happened

• Be curious

These are just recommendations. Consider your own self as you enter this conversation. What more do you need to be your best and bravest self? What would you add to my list?

Imagine if each person in your school or on your job or at your church felt like they could show up as their full self. Imagine how empowering that would feel, instead of the constant pressure to assimilate, to become something you are not. Imagine if we could begin by having the honest conversations needed to articulate what affirming spaces would look like. Imagine what this could do for us in our local communities and at the national level if this—a new way of doing business—became the "norm."

In my own work, I try to model what I ask of my students or my training participants. I do not believe I can ask of others what I am not willing to do myself. I lead with my own vulnerability. Very close to the opening, I share pieces of my story, particularly stories of struggle and overcoming, of WHY the work of racial equity is so important to me. I push through the discomfort that is inevitable when I am presenting to mostly White audiences, many of whom are just beginning their journey into conversations about race and equity.

Sit together now with your group and have a conversation about the kinds of agreements you want to make as a group about how you are going to communicate and move through the work. What will your commitments be to staying in the conversation, even when it becomes particularly uncomfortable or when someone says something (whether intentionally or not) that is offensive? How are you going to be accountable to one another through the process?

If you do not have this conversation, it will be too easy to check out when the conversations are difficult. It will be too easy for people to remain superficial in their conversations and not ever get to the heart of the issues. As a result, the work will stay at the intellectual level and not get to the heart of the issues.

Remember, shame, blame, and guilt are not useful. Acknowledge to yourself and to your partner(s) in the work (if you have one/them) that you are feeling these emotions. Name them and then pivot and back to learning. From thirty years of teaching—in classrooms and at conferences—I have learned that shame and guilt do not actually move learning forward long-term. Shame and guilt may cause change in the short-term, but that change typically does not last, and that change is often just superficial and performative. I encourage attendees—both during class and beyond, as they engage others in-person or on social media—to call people "in" and "up" into their better selves, not "down" and "out" into shame.

Finally, after you have practiced gratitude, established the community agreements you need to encourage brave spaces, I want to encourage you to "ground in." "Grounding-in" is a process of centering ourselves, of focusing on our mental well-being. It is a practice that can be accomplished using various strategies to help individuals develop the state of mind necessary to enter hard conversations. The practice is similar to the breathing exercises women practice in preparation for the birthing process.

The conversations we are about to have regarding your identity and the ways race plays a role in your environments will require you to be in touch with your emotions and be as calm as possible, so you can engage in these conversations in ways that are sustainable. I encourage you to practice "grounding in," not just as you are reading this book but also anytime you are preparing to have a hard conversation—in the context of a training or with a boss or with a teammate or a family member, with a spouse or partner. The more you can make "grounding-in" a natural practice, a habit, the more you will be able to fully participate in critical conversations.

Put down anything in your hands. Sit up as straight as you are able. Plant your feet as firmly on the floor as possible. I always imagine that our feet are connected through the earth in this work. I invite you to close your eyes if you are able and comfortable doing so or find a spot on the wall on which to hyper-focus. Take just thirty seconds to focus completely on the air entering and leaving your body. After thirty seconds, I invite you to stretch, stand up, or do a jumping jack, if that feels right.

I encourage you to practice grounding in beyond a training exercise in this chapter. The next time you read a post on social media that makes you upset and pushes you to be a "thumb-warrior," take thirty seconds or a minute or five (depending upon how problematic the post is). Then go back and decide if you can respond thoughtfully. After looking at other people's responses on the post, make a decision about whether you believe your response is going to be appreciated and valued. I have a rule for myself—"I only have so much energy to put out into the world. I am cautious about where and who gets my energy." There are times when no response is necessary, when silence is what the post deserves.

Imagine if we were all to be more thoughtful and intentional in our responses? Imagine if we did not feel the need to respond in the moment, especially when our emotions were high? Imagine how much more effective our interactions could be if we took time regularly to collect ourselves? Imagine if we actually gave ourselves time to process and reflect on any tough subjects before engaging others with different opinions?

I have come to believe that half our battle in the United States is that we have developed a culture where we just talk... or yell... or shut down on issues that are critical to our health and well-being as a country. If we could develop stronger skills and habits around gratitude and "brave spaces" and grounding-in and then apply those skills any time we are in mixed company or upset or frustrated, we could do the necessary work to move towards healing.

The three practices we have discussed—gratitude, brave spaces, and grounding-in—need to be practiced to the point they are habits, to the point where you develop muscle memory. You do not need to wait for a conversation about race to practice any of them. Instead, seek out opportunities in your home with your children or your partner or on the job with your colleagues to practice each. The more regularly you practice these strategies, the more they will become your "norm," and they will lead you to much more authentic and productive conversations and work.

# 5

# CONTAINERS FOR THE WORK

O ne of the most important classes I took in high school was a public speaking class. Although I had no idea I would eventually become a professional public speaker, there were two elements of the instruction (which was delivered by our then superintendent) that I will hold onto for the rest of my life: 1. KISS (Keep It Simple Stupid), and 2. Have no more than three key points you are going to make, no matter how long your speech is, and use three key words to draw your listener back to those points.

I have always been moved by words. I began to learn my second language, Dutch, when we moved to The Netherlands in 1976. I began to work with two friends in 4th grade to learn Arabic and Hebrew, determined to become a broker of peace between Israel and Palestine somewhere in my distant future. My father took a summer teaching position at a French and Computer camp in Switzerland every summer starting when I was in 6th grade, and I was fairly fluent in French by the time I was twelve years old. As a teen, we would travel as a family and for school athletic trips to other countries in Western Europe regularly. I would sit in the car or bus during those trips, with a phrase book, memorizing phrases I believed would be most useful during my time in whatever country we planned to visit. I had notebooks I carried with me to "hold" the words I found particularly useful and interesting.

When I returned to the United States for college, even though I no longer had opportunities to travel to foreign lands, I was no less interested in the power of words. Although my dean in college encouraged me to stick with just English (I felt an inkling she did not think a Black girl could manage three languages), I was determined to maintain my Spanish and French, so I designed my own major—Literatures of the African Diaspora in English, French and Spanish. As part of my coursework, I took as many linguistics classes as possible. I wanted to understand the foundations of words, what made them work, how one word was connected to another.

My love for language has remained steady. I became an English teacher but then also took on the creation of a middle-level French Immersion program for which I wrote all of the curriculum, including plays and songs and poems. I would perform them for my students, and then we would perform them for others. Although I had been a fairly shy child as a middle school student, teaching middle school forced me to step out of my shell, to embrace my "silly", the actress that had been hiding inside of me.

After leaving the classroom to work in administration, I continued to make presentations. My "students" now were often adults. They were educators in various roles who wanted to learn how to better serve the students I had found success teaching— those who lived in poverty; those who spoke languages other than English at home; those who came from countries with very different education systems; those who came from ethnic backgrounds that were often not visible or celebrated in literature or history textbooks.

Once I became a state executive, I was invited into many spaces to speak on a variety of topics. In 2010, I was invited to speak at a large Martin Luther King, Jr Day event in Seattle. That event would initiate a cascade of new invitations. January remains my busiest public speaking month. I average twenty speaking events over the course of the weeks before and after the national day set aside to recognize this American hero.

I never write speeches. I am a huge believer in being authentic, in speaking to the moment, in speaking from my heart. However, over the course of the many years I have delivered these speeches— now at colleges and businesses and churches, in addition to schools —I have developed a habit of using three words to frame my speech. In 2020, my Martin Luther King, Jr words were "dream," "invest," "love." I encouraged people to think about what dreams they held that could make their world a better place, where they could invest time and energy to become a better version of themselves and how they could learn to (courageously) love those who were most unlike them. By the time we hit April and May and June and had witnessed the murders of Ahmaud Arbery and Breonna Taylor and George Floyd, I was hearing three new words in the wind. These three words have become the framing now for almost every speech I deliver related to race and justice and equity and reconciliation.

Humility. Humanity. History.


## HUMILITY

As someone who ran for office in 2016, during the election cycle that would see Donald Trump elected President, I had the opportunity to be in spaces with very powerful people—both those who were also running for office and those who had already been elected to their positions. I watched with close attention how people engaged one another and how candidates spoke about themselves.

I lost my election by less than 1%. It was a tough loss, but that loss forced me to think deeply about who I was and how I wanted to move through the world and make a difference. The loss forced me to put into practice what I had told my students for decades—"Loss is inevitable. It is just a bump in the road, a change of direction, an opportunity to learn something new; it is not the end."

Losing my election also forced me to embrace humility—the knowledge that I was good, but I was not "all that." That loss also reminded me that, although I could do good things on my own, I could only do great things when working alongside others.

Over the last four, almost five years, I have watched politicians and artists and athletes demonstrate something very different from humility. I have watched the arrogance of national leaders who refuse to listen to those with greater expertise, athletes who think they are immortal, pastors who spoke from pulpits as if they were Jesus, not fallible men with weaknesses and struggles like the masses.

When I look at US, the nation I now call home, I believe one of our greatest weaknesses is our lack of humility. We seem to have an insatiable need to be the greatest, to talk as if we are the best in the world, to be unwilling to be critiqued or to receive constructive criticism from others—those within our borders and those without. I watched the destruction of Colin Kaepernick's football career, as he took a knee and dared call US higher. I watched the rise of #AllLivesMatter and #BlueLivesMatter and the proliferation of alt-right group activity in response to #BlackLivesMatter, who were calling us, as a nation, to grapple with our troubled history of police brutality.

I watched the responses of many as the pandemic shut down our nation and forced each of us to bear witness to the murders of Ahmaud Arbery and Breonna Taylor and George Floyd. I watched predominantly White crowds march state capitols brandishing weapons demanding the opening of businesses and the discontinuation of mask requirements—"How dare you infringe upon my rights as a citizen!"

I suddenly had this realization, after living in the United States for over thirty years: being required to wear a mask, being asked to stay home for the health of others, must be what oppression feels like to people who have never experienced oppression.

I witnessed former members of our predominantly White evangelical church post online about the evils of a government that would not allow churches to meet in person. They insisted the stay-home orders were intentionally anti-Christian. They insisted anyone who wore a mask was complicit. Masks and staying at home were politicized in ways I had not imagined.

And I was drawn back to a passage from the Bible that had moved me to write a song many years before: "If my people, who are called by my name, will HUMBLE themselves and pray and seek my face and turn from their wicked ways, then I will hear from heaven, and I will forgive their sin and will heal their land." 2 Chronicles 7:14

I was a panelist for a Zoom Town Hall devoted to how different faith communities were moving through this "pandemic moment." I thought about my own (Christian) faith community. Many had marched on our Washington State Capitol and were posting regularly about how unfair government mandates were. During the Town Hall, I listened to the leader of the Muslim community in Tacoma talk about how in his faith they were expected to pray together shoulder-to-shoulder (physically touching one another), and how the 6' distance requirements had forced them to rethink how they practiced their faith.

No complaining.

No argument that the government was intentionally targeting Muslims.

I was moved by the imam's description of the attitude of his community (who were often vilified for other reasons) and their willingness to adapt and adjust.

Humility. His words reminded me that we, as a nation, lack humility.

Although websites and blogs were popping up across social media claiming either the pandemic was a hoax, created by the

Chinese or created by Democrats seeking to unseat a President, OR claiming to have cures to COVID19, it was obvious to me, even watching national leaders in the medical industry, NO ONE knew exactly how to respond to the pandemic.

As protests erupted across the nation, and then across the globe, in support of Black Lives Matter, I realized that, similar to the response to the health pandemic, no one really knew "the answers" to "fixing racism" in the United States, either. People were joining Zoom book clubs right and left, reading Dr. Ibrahim X. Kendi to learn about anti-racism and Robin DiAngelo to learn about white fragility. No single person had "the answer" for our ills.

As much as I would have liked to have created a road map to "fix" racism in the United States, I realized in the midst of the pandemic, I was just one piece of a solution. As much of my life as I have devoted to helping students become their best selves and helping teachers more effectively engage diverse populations of students, I did not have all the answers, either. There was so much work to be done, and there was room for many of us to do it. No single person had all the answers.

I hold such a small piece of the solution.

I know some things having lived in my Black and White skin for fifty years. More importantly, I can do nothing great on my own. I need to link arms with others who are also doing this work.

And so I engaged with others every day over the last fifteen months. I hosted weekly gatherings on Zoom. I joined a group called the Equity Institute, a collaborative of other consultants and educators and community advocates equally passionate about this work. I hold space every Saturday afternoon for Black and Brown and Native educators who need a space to just be, to vent or lament about the current state of affairs. I participate with other educators in weekly gatherings of students of color and students who identify as LGBTQIA in order to create space for them to process identity and current events. In those spaces, I am both facilitator and learner.

## HUMANITY

From the election of President Trump through the election of President Biden, I watched US denigrate "other," whoever that might be at the moment. I watched Republicans call Democrats "baby-killers" and "Marxists." I watched Democrats call Republicans "racists" and "idiots." I watched Black people and their allies take to the streets in support of Black Lives Matter, and I watched the Proud Boys and other alt-right groups show up in protest. I heard from Black students who tried to convene Black Student Union meetings that were Zoom-bombed by others yelling racial epithets and telling them to go back to Africa. I heard from Asian students who had been called names in the chat sections of their school Zoom meetings and accused of bringing the Corona Virus to America.

I watched the police and National Guard responses to Black Lives Matter protests across the nation. I witnessed my own daughter sprayed in the face with tear gas by a police officer as she tried to help a White woman up off the ground after she was trampled at the end of a peaceful protest in Seattle. I watched the ways that those in authority dehumanized those they were supposed to be protecting, and I heard citizens on the ground vilifying all police.

In recent weeks, I witnessed the trial of Derek Chauvin, the police officer who was recently convicted for the murder of George Floyd. During the three weeks of the trial, pictures circulated again of Floyd's final moments of life as he gasped for air with a police officer's full weight on his neck. I never watched the video, but the photo of Chauvin said it all. The look in his eyes, his stance, reminded me of the photos I had seen of my father and his brother after killing a deer in the woods of Northern Minnesota. They would stand over the dead carcass with their rifles, proud of having conquered the beast.

The photograph of Derek Chauvin atop George Floyd will

forever live in my memory as a powerful representation of dehumanization.

As I watched US denigrate one another in very explicit ways over the last year, I was drawn to the idea that our only way forward is not necessarily to agree with one another but to find ways to disagree while centering the "other's" humanity. It became apparent that we were no longer seeing "other" as deserving of the same dignity as whoever we considered to be a member of "our community."

It is easy to call a fellow citizen the "n-word" when you do not see them as your equal. It is easy to call your neighbor a "baby-killer" when you do not see them as being "made in the image of God."

Our only way forward to healing seems to rest in our willingness to humanize the people around us, even and especially those who look and sound and believe differently from us. I make every effort to go out of my way to get curious about people who say things that are in stark contrast to what I believe. My rule for myself has become, "When they say that thing that makes you mad, Erin, get curious. Ask why they believe that thing, how they came to that conclusion."

Giving myself permission to get curious instead of angry was so useful. On social media, instead of starting by trying to educate a person out of their (flawed) belief, I began to ask questions, to try to get to the bottom of how they developed that belief in the first place. I made the conscious choice to imagine them as a member of my family and to show up to them as someone who really wanted to get to know them more authentically, not as someone who was there to "get them straight."

That change in attitude set me free and allowed me to show up in ways that were healthier, and, in the end, much more effective. I even learned new things about myself and broadened my own thinking on issues with which I had little previous exposure.

HISTORY

We each have a history to consider. All of our stories contain good, bad and ugly. You read elements of my story in Chapter 2. You have a story as well—the ways your identities have informed how you move through the world, the ways where you lived and around whom changed how you experienced this country.

Every community has a history. For example, our state Capitol, Olympia, was originally a Whites-only city. The state of Oregon was designed as a state for only White people. Many members of the Indigenous communities here in Washington State, but also across the nation, were forced to attend boarding schools, where they were stripped of their languages and cultural practices up until a generation before mine. Although those realities have changed legally, there are consequences for these origin stories. These histories have implications for how communities experience the state of Washington and the United States today.

As a former history teacher, I believe the United States has developed a habit of telling history in a selective way. We elevate certain stories in which "we" are the hero and ignore stories in which we are the villain. The full history must be told and faced, or there cannot be healing. Putting a band-aid over a gaping wound does not allow it to heal. In fact, beneath that covering, no matter how pretty the design on the plaster, the wound festers. We see evidence of the festering now.

Similar to the stories of community, there are also stories of institutions. All of the major institutions in our country have histories influenced by race—education, health care, housing, voting and policing to name a few. Different groups have had different levels and types of access to systems at different times in our history. We cannot go back and change what was before, but we can make sure going forward we acknowledge the harm and the ways that harm continues to have an impact today. We can consider ways to repair the harm and provide increased and accelerated access wherever possible.

I tell my personal (her)story in hundreds of spaces every year. I do not tell it to brag or to seek out the sympathy of others. I tell my story to connect to others, hoping each person who hears my story will find something in it that aligns to their personal story. I tell my story to model vulnerability, to encourage listeners to be vulnerable and authentic in their own telling of stories. I tell my story hoping it will encourage listeners to get curious about others who have stories significantly different from theirs. I tell my story to challenge listeners to realize there is still so much work to be done.

If we are going to move forward in ways that lead us all to flourishing, we must be willing to tell and listen to personal stories, stories of community, histories of organizations, histories of regions and of our nation. Without truly facing our past and holding ourselves accountable for the ways we have done harm, we cannot move forward into the best versions of ourselves.

Humility. Humanity. History.

# 6

# GETTING ON THE SAME PAGE

Much of the work of race and equity is about language. We often throw around language, assuming everyone has the same definitions or that people are familiar with the language we use (which seems to be constantly shifting). In this chapter, I hope to find some common ground on how we communicate with regards to words like "equity," "equality," "diversity," "inclusion," and the many others I have come across in my time as an educator. I believe that how we speak about these things, especially in the education sector, has a tremendous impact on how we interact with and support each other as well as shape the world for our students.

Although I knew that I wanted to be a teacher by the beginning of my sophomore year of college, Bryn Mawr had no teacher education program. I began volunteering in a school in Philadelphia, which opened my eyes to dramatic differences in expectations and opportunities in that context. When I joined my husband in South Bend, Indiana, and began to substitute teach in the public schools there, where bussing had just begun in the 80s, I witnessed the tensions created when inner-city Black students were bussed to a suburban predominantly White community. Once again, I saw differences in expectations and opportunities.

I did not have language for any of the things I was seeing or experiencing. I just knew the public education system was incredibly flawed. I knew inherently that race and zip code played a massive role in who flourished, who had access to better materials and more rigor, who was expected to fail, and who was assumed to be without potential.

It was not until I earned my graduate-level teaching certificate in Tacoma, WA, and began teaching in Title I schools that I began to see the ways systems worked (or didn't) and began to hear language that resonated with me. My first full-time teaching job was in a middle school in Tacoma that had just fallen into "failing" status and required support from the State Superintendent's Office. I did not even know what "requiring school improvement" meant at the time, but even as a first-year teacher, I knew I wanted to learn more. So I showed up at the first School Improvement Committee meeting. When the principal asked who on staff would be willing to be the leader of the work of "improvement," no one wanted the job.

Finally, I raised my hand. Having just earned my teaching certificate eight months earlier, I became the staff lead for our school improvement work. I had no idea what the work of School Improvement would entail, but I have always been one who embraces a challenge, especially if it means my work will help the community move in a positive direction. What I did not know was that my YES meant I would be invited to regular meetings with state education leaders. What I did not know was that for three summers in a row, I would be invited to a school improvement summit hosted by the State Superintendent herself. What I did not know was that I would be introduced to words like "diversity" and "the achievement gap" and "cultural competence."

I began to have regular conversations with staff about data. We looked at disaggregated data to consider how Black students were experiencing over-representation in discipline data but under-representation in access to advanced courses. We began to look at how many Black and Native students were recommended for Special

60

Education services versus how many White and Asian students were invited to test into the Highly Capable programs. These things were representations of "the achievement gap"—the ways students of color, particularly Black, Latinx and Native students were under-performing their White peers.

In my last year at the middle school, I also took on the role as Director for the Act Six Program, a program that supported a cohort of Tacoma area students who were primarily Black, Pacific Islander, Latinx, Native and Southeast Asian and the first in their families to attend college. In their senior year of high school, I trained these students once a week in the skills they would need to survive on the predominantly White, middle-class campus of Whitworth University, a small Christian liberal arts college in Spokane, WA. We had conversations weekly about the differences in opportunities these students had in high school and how we needed to prepare them to match their White peers in their ability to critique litera-ture and write at the college level. We also talked at length about significant differences in culture and language. We talked about the college's work to develop skills to embrace new cultural expressions to create an inclusive empowering environment for these students. This is how I came to better understand what was meant by "cul-tural competence"— knowledge of the ways different cultural groups express themselves. I learned about the importance of helping organizations (including schools) look intentionally at the cultural norms by which they were expecting people to operate to determine if they were affirming various cultures or requiring everyone to assimilate to one set of expectations.

My husband, our three children, and I moved to Spokane to follow our students at the end of that year. He took a job as the director of a para-church organization on the North end of Spokane. I was hired as a literacy instructional coach for a school in the same community, where the population was primarily White and almost all living below the poverty line.

In that context, we talked about the realities of poverty and the limitations poverty created around access to academic programs and high expectations. As an instructional coach, I had the opportunity to sit in administrative meetings as conversations were had about culture in the building and how we could raise our expectations and the levels of rigor for our students while also providing students with the levels of support—academic, social and physical —they needed to get the most out of their school experiences. I had the opportunity to develop training for adults to help them serve students who were not experiencing success in school spaces.

I earned the Milken Educator of the Year for Washington State in my second year at the high school. I believe this award came because of the ways I helped the school think about "closing gaps," particularly for our most marginalized students; my creation of a girls group for the small group of Black and Brown girls in our building; as well as the development of a clothing closet to support the many families who experienced evictions, homelessness or who needed a professional outfit to attend a job interview. I will never know for sure how I won that award because it is a complete surprise. Someone in your building must make an application on your behalf. You are not aware of the award until a surprise assembly at your school where the Milken Family Foundation presents the award. Several months later, you and your spouse are flown to Los Angeles for a red carpet event, where you receive a $25,000 check you can use in any way you please.

The very same State Superintendent who had facilitated the three years of school improvement work I had done in my previous middle school happened to show up in Los Angeles at the red carpet event. Her presence opened a new door, one that would propel me from the school building to the state government working as the Director for the Center for the Improvement of Student Learning. This office served all school districts in the state to provide training and resources to more effectively support students of color and students whose families spoke a language other than English in the home.

Although I have been doing bridge-building work naturally most of my life and have cared about the role of race and justice in education spaces since my first visit to a poor, 100% Black school in Philadelphia in 1990, I was not someone who would have referred to "racial equity," even ten years ago when I first took the director position at the state. I did not get into the work by doing graduate studies in social justice or by studying critical race theory. I came to the work of racial equity and justice through my own experiences as an educator and as the mother of Black children. I was propelled formally into the professional work of racial equity as tends to happen most in my life—by being in places where justice was needed. I have always seen open doors as an opportunity and walked through them.

When I first arrived at the State Superintendent's Office, we talked a LOT about diversity. At the time, what we meant by "diversity" was merely "people of color." We were asking ourselves, "How are people of color experiencing school spaces?"

Through the work I did to support families and to help schools effectively engage often marginalized families, I had the opportunity to connect with schools in various communities across our state—from large urban school districts with dozens of languages spoken to small, rural bilingual communities in Eastern Washington. I had the opportunity to be in spaces with both families and educators. Meanwhile, I was parenting three Black teenagers and experiencing my own challenges—how I was being treated as a parent, how my children were treated, and how race and culture were being addressed... or not.

My office provided training and support to schools with "diverse" student populations. We provided online tools for "diverse" families to better navigate school spaces. Through this process, we began to talk about "cultural competence," the idea that educators could develop broader understandings of the different cultural norms of the students and communities they were serving. We talked about different cultural communication styles and values. We talked a lot about the importance of having interpreters at every meeting and making sure all materials were translated into at least the primary languages spoken in each building.

Having lived in two countries and visited twelve others, I have more expansive knowledge than most of a variety of cultures and cultural norms. I was an expert in the "ways" of White middle-class people because I had been raised in White middle-class spaces by White middle-class people. As a result, I was able to serve as a bridge to help educators (who are predominantly White and female in the state of Washington) communicate more effectively with students and families with different communication styles and cultural norms.

However, over time, as I transitioned from Director to Assistant State Superintendent and entered the world of policy, I realized all of our work around "cultural competence" was not enough to move the needle in any significant way. First of all, "cultural competence" suggests a person can become "competent," as if there is an "end" somehow to the learning cycle as if someone can develop an awareness of all the elements of every culture. That was an impossible task.

I also realized over time that just understanding the different cultural elements did not change systems. Although families may have felt more welcome in buildings, just ensuring clear communication was not making the kinds of substantial changes in schools required for students to reach their full potential. Understanding cultural norms also did not change test scores or graduation rates, which was our charge at the State Superintendent's Office. What was actually required was an honest and thorough interrogation of systems to determine what was working or not working and for whom.

This is where the word "equity" entered our lexicon. Equity is not equality. Equity is not about giving every student or building the same thing, which is typically what happens in school spaces and government programs. Equity is about taking down barriers and/or building the bridges necessary for all stakeholders to THRIVE. Although there are various ways to look at equity—gender, socioeconomic background, language—in my work, I focus intentionally on racial equity because it has been my experience that we have the hardest time talking about race as a nation. I have a practice of trying the hard thing first. This—RACE—is a hard thing. Talking about race will be uncomfortable, but with all that we learn about racial equity, you will be able to apply it to other identities, as you need.

Over time I learned to see "diversity" as more than race or ethnicity. I learned to see "diversity" as the many ways students (or whoever your constituents or clients are) are different. Diversity is also expressed in the ways we choose to celebrate those differences with an event, like Black History Month or Pride. However, acknowledging and even celebrating "diversity" is a beginning step, not an end. Recognizing diversity in a space does not actually change that space in any significant way.

Although I began talking and training on "cultural competence," we transitioned in the last four years to talking about "culturally responsive practice" to be proactive, continuously, and consistently responsive to the different cultural values and expressions that should be considered in classrooms and workspaces. "Culturally responsive practice" means considering the different cultural expressions and ways of being that exist within a classroom, institution or organization and choosing to intentionally adopt cultural practices that affirm all who are members of that community. "Culturally responsive practices" are critical to creating inclusive spaces. However, as important as those practices are, they are limited to a room, office, or building. These practices alone do not change systems.

Committing to equity is the only way we will create the kinds of substantive, sustainable changes that lead to all people flourishing. Equity requires unpacking all the ways race is implicated in systems, practices, and policies. We must consider the ways policies and practices are developed and implemented and then use our power, voices, and influence to stop harmful practices and institute practices that ensure the support that leads to the thriving of all people in our community and our nation.

As someone who has been a world language teacher, I want to invite you into an opportunity to learn and become fluent in this new language. As with most languages, the lexicon will change over time. You will need to adapt and adjust as we learn new things and get better in this work. We move to more asset-based language and get clearer about what is actually needed to allow more people in the United States to experience flourishing. Give yourself grace when you get a term wrong. I am still learning myself.

# 7

# MOVES TO GET TO EQUITY

O ver the last year, I have been in dozens of rooms listening to decision-makers talk about racial equity and social justice. In most of those spaces, leaders want support to develop an "equity statement" or create a job description for a new Director of Equity (which they know they should have but are often unsure of what the role should do). I have heard school board members, superintendents, and non-profit executive directors talk about having an equity policy.

However, I have come to believe that people cannot write an effective policy statement, nor should they hire a Director of Equity, if they have not done some significant self-work to determine how their own identities have informed how they understand and move through the world. They also cannot effectively do the work of equity if they do not have a more intimate knowledge of their students, clients, or constituents' identities and stories. They need to be willing to confront who they are serving well and who is not being served well. They must consider who is missing at decision-making tables, and how they could build stronger relationships with members of that community to ensure the policy and practices encourage and allow particular groups to flourish, not further contributing to their oppression.

I spent most of my in-classroom career working in Title I buildings. These are the poorest buildings in the nation, the ones in which most children qualify for free-and-reduced lunch. The greatest challenge in these spaces was always the overwhelming number of conversations between adults about testing, the pressure to get all students in the building to "meet or exceed standard" (arbitrary measurements of progress determined by people often not representative of the students I served). Some charter schools compensate teachers for their ability to "get students to standard." However, traditional public schools face the pressure of the public, the pressure of the narrative that because your school is a "failing school," because your students are "failing," you, as an educator, must not be trying hard enough.

I taught in four middle schools in Tacoma and a high school in Spokane. All five buildings were deemed "failing schools" at some point by the state of Washington. I want you to imagine what it feels like as a teacher to know you are in a "failing" school, the pressure exerted explicitly and subtly to make sure your students are up-to-speed and have been prepared well enough for the annual state test. I want you to imagine being a student in that building, always hearing whispers of your "failing" status, the abundance of deficit thinking.

I felt the pressure to prepare my students for standardized tests like everyone else. Even in my first year of teaching in Washington State, when I was asked to take over a classroom as the long-term substitute for a teacher who was having a baby, I felt incredible pressure to help her students meet standards on a test I had never seen. In my first year as a full-time teacher, I was at the school with the most students living in poverty. My students did not have consistent housing or food. I was still trying to figure out teaching, and now I would have to prepare them for a test I did not fully understand myself.

I began to feel the realities of our propensity in education to lean towards equality, not equity. With no additional resources or supports, how were children in communities where many parents worked multiple jobs just to pay the bills or children who were just learning to speak English because they had recently immigrated to the country, expected to reach the same standards as children in homes where parents made six figures and could afford piano lessons, summer camps, tutoring? How could teachers in neighborhoods where students were living in poverty make the same salaries as teachers in wealthier communities and be expected (without additional compensation) to do all necessary to fill in the gaps? Did not equity require doing something different, meeting students and families where they were, and providing them with whatever was necessary to get them to "thriving"?

I will never forget the following year, my first year teaching French Immersion at Stewart Middle School. I was teaching every subject in French without any instruction in English, so I assumed my sixth-grade students would not test with their English-only peers. That made sense to me. Our state's test was not written in French, and my students were learning exclusively in French. How could they be expected to take a test in English then?

That assumption gave me a sense of freedom. Instead of feeling pressure to jump straight into content on the first day, I tried new things with students. I decided to spend the first three weeks of the school year in English just doing team-building activities. My gut told me that if these students, most of whom had never heard French before, were going to be learning in only French, they would need to trust one another, and they would need to trust me. We were going to need to build a solid community. On that foundation, I could lay new vocabulary and grammatical structures, as well as improved science and math content.

After three weeks, I transitioned to French-only.

The first month with no English was hard for students. They were frustrated—with me, with themselves. Some stayed completely quiet and would not engage verbally at all. Others committed to spending hours at home watching their favorite Disney films in French so they could become familiar more quickly with the sounds of the language. Some used art to create depictions of complex concepts. Others developed their own board and card games to teach themselves and others.

Although this school was one of the poorest in our city and most of the students were students of color, I saw brilliance in each one of them. They may not have been able to formulate much that was intelligible in French by Winter Break, but they could all understand close to 90% of my instructions by that point. I hoped that students would be able to accelerate that learning through the second semester when we returned from break.

Winter break ended, and the first semester came to a close. My students had already passed many English-only students in the content they had learned, even though we had started with team building instead of core content like the rest of the school. My assumptions had been correct—if they could learn to trust and depend on one another, deep learning would take place.

One day, during the first or second week of February, my principal came into the room to see me. I had a practice of not speaking English to anyone who entered my classroom during the school day, even if that person spoke no French at all. All my principal could say was, "oui, oui" and "bonjour," which he used excessively (he had fun pretending). At times, he would speak English, and I would respond back in French. A student would translate for him. At times, if students were working on an assignment, I would respond to him in writing (English).

On this particular day, the principal was making rounds to check on teachers' standardized test preparation processes. Every teacher had been given a stack of preparation materials to use once or twice a week in preparation for the state test, which would happen at the beginning of April. He had brought me a box of prep material, which was, of course, in English. I looked at him quizzically, assuming he was mistaken in bringing these materials to my classroom.

"Pourquoi?" I asked.

A student translated, "Why?"

"Well, you need to get your students ready for the state test."

"Pourquoi?" I asked again.

"Your students will be testing with all the other students."

"En français?" I asked.

That he understood. "No. In English."

Huh?! That made no sense at all. Why would I take time out of my limited schedule to prepare students for a test in a language in which they were receiving no instruction?

"Your students will be testing. So, will the Japanese students and the Spanish students."

I was so angry. No one had ever said anything about the state test. I had come so far with my students. I was afraid that switching into English now would send my students backwards. I was not about to go backwards after all the work we had done.

I did not let my students see my emotion. Instead, we continued with our daily activities.

This experience represents one of the most significant challenges of how public education is designed. So much of schooling is based on equality—the notion that every child must DO the same things—instead of equity—the idea that students should get whatever they need to thrive.

It was obvious to me that my students were learning. They demonstrated this learning in my classroom every day, even if it was in French and in a way that a state test could not measure. I had already been considering a different way to measure my students' growth. In fact, several of us who were teaching immersion in my district and others were in the process of developing a tool that would help us evaluate our students' learning.

When I returned home that night, I shared the news with my husband. "Honey, I can't believe I am going to have to test my students. This is so unfair." And then I had a revelation. "You know what? I don't think I am going to prepare them at all. Maybe they will all fail, but I think I am going to trust my gut. My gut said at the beginning of the year to have them just focus on becoming a team. I am going to trust that my belief in them and their belief in themselves will be enough. If they fail, they fail. If I get fired because of that, oh, well."

By the way, according to the documentation I had received about my students prior to the first day of class, 30% of them had entered my classroom reading and doing math at third or fourth-grade levels. I chose not to pay any attention to those scores. I chose to believe each of my students was brilliant and to treat them as such.

We never did touch those test preparation packets, and my students would take the state test just months later. Every one of them met or exceeded state standards, as did the students from the Japanese and Spanish Immersion classrooms. What I learned through that experience was:

1. The state test does not necessarily tell us much about our students.
2. Students will rise to whatever standard you set for them, so set the bar high and then provide them with high levels of support, and
3. More important than preparing students with content knowledge is preparing them to believe in themselves and think critically.

What does that have to do with equity?

After years of teaching in classrooms just like this one, I would be propelled into work at the state level, where I was expected to make decisions about policy and practice. My experiences in the classroom, my practice of giving students not the same things but whatever I thought they needed to thrive, helped me think differently about my work at the next level. My position as a Director for the State Superintendent began just after President Obama had taken office. At the time, many educators and political pundits were talking about eliminating the "Achievement Gap." Unfortunately, there was a considerable focus on comparing the scores of students by racial group, with White students always being the standard.

The state of Washington was not serving Black, Native and Latinx students well, based on the scores we saw across the board. A committee was developed at the state level called the Achievement Gap Oversight and Accountability Committee. Its sole focus was to develop strategies to serve students of color more effectively. As the Director of the Center for the Improvement of Student Learning, one of my jobs was to facilitate this state-level committee that had representation from each of the four non-White racial groups and a handful of state legislators who could consider considering this the legislative implications for our learning.

I was one of the only executives at the Superintendent's Office who had come directly out of a classroom, unlike many who had served as building principals or district administrators before they went to the state capitol. So much of what people talked about was theoretical. It was located in the text of a doctoral thesis or a research paper. I was coming into space as a practitioner, one who had been pretty successful in spaces that were often written off as "failing."

Every time I heard the phrase "achievement gap," something tightened in my stomach. Every time someone talked about the "achievement gap," they criticized Black, Brown, or Native students; their families and communities; or the educators who served them. That did not feel right to me at all. Remember, I had spent my career serving "those" students. I was "that" parent. My children were "those" children. I witnessed the extraordinary efforts of teachers and para educators and counselors in "those" buildings. I was the teacher who stayed up until midnight writing lesson plans, who drove to the home of a student to make sure they had new shoes or a backpack. I had spent years in the presence of young people who were brilliant and talented but who often didn't "show up" that way on standardized tests.

The more I sat in spaces with education leaders and decision-makers, the more I realized we were missing the mark somehow. At the same time, I experienced my own children move through public education. My youngest son, who taught himself to read at three years old and to do math (multiplication) at five years old, tested to be admitted for entrance into the gifted program. He was accused by a district administrator of cheating on the test (in front of a group of adults and children and me).

"You couldn't have scored this high on your own," the administrator said.

My son was the only Black child testing that day.

I wanted to say, "You cannot imagine a large Black boy can be smart?!"

Before I could "reach out and touch" this administrator, my fabulous on-the-spectrum, twice-exceptional child responded, "I will just retake the test and score higher, Sir."

I witnessed my youngest son's academic brilliance time and time again, despite what the education system "expected" of a large Black boy.

I watched our adopted daughter, who had lost her mother as a nine-year-old and whose father was serving a thirty-year prison sentence, memorize and perform soliloquies in front of her peers with flawless precision. I watched her walk across the graduation stage at Central Washington University, having already been published in an academic journal. I watched my oldest son rehearse to perform an operetta in Latin at Carnegie Hall at four-teen years old and then be invited to audition for The Voice, shortly after opening the State Legislature singing the National Anthem a cappella. From the time he was six years old, he spent hours sharing the statistics of players from different sports—from basketball to football to rugby to baseball—and yet he was called stupid three different times in his K-12 career by teachers who worked with him, because of his dysgraphia and inability to write legibly.

My children are fabulous because they are mine. I do not believe they are exceptional. I think, far too often, we have written off little Black boys and little Black girls in our language about them and in our expectations for them. The mere use of the phrase "achievement gap" suggests that we expect less from children who look like mine.

I found myself sitting in meetings wondering if "opportunity" was not a more appropriate way to talk about what students needed. Were Black and Brown and Native students not meeting standards on state tests, not graduating on time, not entering and completing college because they just didn't have the "right" opportunities? This sounded better to me at the time. This put the onus on the system to provide the necessary support instead of blaming children or individual teachers for their inability to perform on a test. I began to call the problem we were trying to address the "opportunity gap," instead of the "achievement gap." That felt more fair and accurate.

After just over a year at the State Superintendent's Office as a Director, I was promoted to Assistant State Superintendent. This meant I now had new responsibilities, one of which was to head up the street to the Capitol to testify on education bills. As I entered the hearing rooms, because I facilitated the Achievement Gap Oversight and Accountability Committee, there was usually at least one familiar face smiling back at me.

Over my three years as Assistant State Superintendent, I developed relationships with many Senators and State Representatives. Each one who served had great intentions and wanted to use their influence to impact their constituents' lives positively. However, as I watched lawmakers interact during hearings and then inside conference rooms and then on the House and Senate floors, some things became abundantly clear. Most decision-makers were White people, primarily male. Most were of the age that their children were already out of school. Most, it seemed, did not have authentic, meaningful relationships with Black and Brown and Native people. Why did this matter? When they wrote law and policy, they did so not based on what they knew students of color needed but what they thought students of color might need, often in response to "this" new study or "that" packet of data from a state or local research organization.

I began to realize that even "opportunity gap" was not enough to address the educational needs of Black, Brown, and Native students. The kinds of changes we needed to see were not going to happen just because those students and their communities had more opportunities. Opportunities were just a fraction of the solution. The reality is that systems—education, healthcare, transportation—were created to serve White, middle-class people. Many of our largest systems were made and designed for the 1900s, when Black, Native, and Latinx people would not have had access to them. Our greatest challenge as a country is that we have not honestly interrogated these systems, now that our realities are different, to determine where policy, procedures, and practices may create barriers for specific populations. We have not considered, on a systemic level, where certain structures need to be abolished entirely or significantly changed to better serve populations for whom these systems were not originally intended.

This is where I began to hear and understand the role of "equity." Equity is about thriving, not just surviving. Equity requires interrogating the systems at play to determine where there are walls that need to be torn down and where there are bridges that need to be built to connect people to resources and opportunities.

Even once decision-makers began to use the term "equity" to create offices of "Equity and Diversity" or "Diversity, Equity and Inclusion," I realized too often government agencies and nonprofits and schools were trying to get to equity by immediately writing an equity policy or developing a new hiring process to recruit and retain more people of color. However, because decision-makers had little to no connection with the people who were most disenfranchised and minoritized by systems, they were often writing these policies and developing these processes in ways that were not helpful and, on occasion, did greater harm.

The more I sat in meetings listening to decision-makers try to come up with the best solutions for people of color, the more I realized that getting to equity would require people to move through three phases:

1. Understand the role your personal identities and personal story play in how you understand and move through the world and experience systems;

2. Understand the ways Black, Brown, and Native people move differently through the world and through the systems you are hoping to affect, and develop the kinds of authentic relationships necessary to learn about the changes they want and need;

3. Interrogate the systems at play that have created barriers for some and opportunities for others and develop new policies and practices WITH people who have traditionally not been at the table.

In the following chapters, I will break down how I help people move through these three cycles. I want to invite you not to rush, not to move quickly through cycle one and cycle two so that you can get to the "fixes." You will not be able to effectively fix anything if you do not first do your own self-work. Take your time. It has taken us generations to get to where we are. We will not change our current reality by jumping ahead and not building a strong foundation to lay those critical changes.

8

# UNPACKING PERSONAL STORY

Your personal story is critical to the conversation about racial equity and racial justice. You bring a lifetime of experiences and perspectives that matter so much in this work. We are about to have an honest conversation about the elements of identity and personal narrative I believe to be most important to consider in this work.

I have always been told I look younger than I am, but I am definitely feeling fifty. When I do not feel it in my joints, my eyes are now reminding me of the effects of aging. What was once 20/20 vision is now waning. All the time in front of a screen during the pandemic has had an observable impact on these eyes and has exacerbated the natural consequences of the aging process.

That being said, my present need for reading glasses and "blue light" glasses (which I use when I know I will need to be on-screen for several hours at a time) have provided me with a new perspective that is incredibly helpful in thinking about the topic of racial equity. The reality is that we all have lenses through which we see the world around us, through which we understand and make meaning of our world, whether we wear glasses or contacts or continue to have 20/20 vision.

This acknowledgment of our lenses is critical to effective work in the area of racial equity. My experience over years of doing this work is that the most "dangerous" people, who do the most harm, are not those who set out to harm or who are mean-spirited. Instead, the most dangerous people are those who do not think they have a perspective, who think the way they see and experience the world is "normal," just like everyone else.

Each of us has been influenced by the identities we carry—both the identities that are visible to others and those that are not so visible but are a function of experiences and encounters and personal decisions (by us and by those around us). Each of us is influenced by the skin in which we were born, our ethnic heritage (if we have or know of one), the culture in which we were raised, our gender (both how we experience ourselves and how others perceive us), our age, our abilities, our socioeconomic background, our family structure, any faith or spiritual beliefs we may espouse and political affiliations. All of these things inform how we show up every day in the world and how the world shows up to us.

Why is it important to understand the lenses we wear, the perspectives we hold? Because it is through those lenses that we make determinations about what is fair and just, who is valuable and who is not, whether we think it our responsibility to engage on issues of justice or believe it is not our place, whether we can assume we have answers to critical problems or believe we need a network of others to make difficult decisions.

All too often, those in positions of authority have been able to move through the world without interrogating their identities. Their identities have "worked" for them. Their identities have not created barriers, and so they have moved through the world, assuming the same is true for others.

"If they would just work as hard as I did, they would experience the same success."

"If they would just learn to speak English better, they would be more accepted."

"If they would wear their hair differently, they would get hired."

"If they would.."

As we consider racial equity, I want to focus this conversation on my own journey to understand my racial identity.

I was born brown out of the body of a White woman. White people adopted me. Although our family lived in Stillwater, Minnesota for the first five years of my life, and my racial identity was ALWAYS a "thing" (not always negative, but it was always noticed), once we moved to The Netherlands, nobody asked why my parents were White while I was Black.

I was Erin, daughter of Bruce and Dorothy Adamson, beloved teachers in my private American school.

Who are the people who birthed and raised you? How have their identities shaped the person you are today?

I will never forget the first year there were Black students in my school. It was seventh grade. Ronnie and Dawn showed up on the first day of school. Both of their parents were in the military and had been stationed at a nearby base. Dawn was tall like me. Ronnie was tiny. We were IMMEDIATELY connected. I cannot even explain to you how that happened, but I knew the instant I saw them, we needed to be connected, and we were. Dawn and I were the "Twin Towers" on the basketball court. Off the court, we were the three amigas. We were inseparable.

Until that encounter, I did not realize I was missing anything. I felt different in my school, not because of my color but because I was one of the only "not rich" kids. The school was very expensive. Most of the students around me lived in mansions (well, they felt like mansions, compared to our tiny apartment). I was the teachers' kid who attended the expensive private school for free.

That year I heard "Black music" for the first time. Of course, I had heard Stevie Wonder and Michael Jackson and Whitney Houston before, but that was mainstream music. That was "everybody" music. I remember the first time I heard the smooth tones of George Benson at Ronnie's house. Although my parents had exposed me to a wide variety of music, I had never heard anything like what Ronnie and Dawn's parents played in their homes. I loved every song! I could feel a connection to the sounds and rhythms deep in my soul.

Ronnie's mom hot-combed my hair for the first time to make it straight, and then at the end of 8th grade, she gave me my first chemical relaxer to straighten my hair. If there was anything I did not like about myself, it was not my skin color; it was my kinky hair. In the days of Charlie's Angels, long and straight, with feathered bangs, was the norm. My kinky, curly hair could not do that. I hoped that I could make my hair look like everyone else's in my school with a relaxer.

I remember the burning sensation on the back of my head as the chemicals ate into my scalp. The longer Ronnie's mom could leave the chemicals on my hair, she told me, the straighter it would become. I could take a little discomfort for that. That burning would leave scabs on my scalp for weeks. I do not know that my skin ever fully healed from those chemical burns, but that was a price I was willing to pay at the time to "fit in."

I got to high school, and both of the girls moved away. There were two older Black boys, but that was it in my school freshman year. Although I felt drawn to those boys, they were very wealthy and very much out of my league. Later a new group of Black students moved into the area from a military base an hour and a half from school. There still was never talk about skin color. No one in my school or community ever talked about race. What was more important in that context was nationality. "What country are you from?" people would ask.

Where are the places you saw yourself represented? Were there more people around you who were like you, or were you an "outsider" somehow? Did you see yourself reflected in the faces of your teachers and coaches and doctors and local leaders?

I spoke Dutch and French fairly fluently by high school, so when we traveled, unlike many of the other American students, I was "nationally ambiguous." I could literally be from anywhere. I made the choice not to speak English in public. Wherever I was, I endeavored to speak the language of that environment. Although I was never fluent in German, I could speak German enough to manage basic conversations if we were in Germany or Austria, or Switzerland. I was like a chameleon.

Sophomore year of high school, my father decided to take me on a school-sponsored trip to the United States with an organization called Close Up in DC. The trip is designed for sophomores in high school to spend a week on Capitol Hill visiting important government sites, meeting politicians and lawmakers, and participating in mock debates. My father had taken a group the year before and thought this would be a good experience for me, mainly because Minnesota was the only place I had ever been in the United States.

Nine other students traveled with us. We were set to spend a week in DC and then a week in New York City. Our school was one of several international schools that participated in this particular session. We would be joined by several public schools from across the United States. The hope was that we would develop an interest in the political process and grow from this cultural exchange.

We flew from Schipol Airport in Amsterdam to Dulles International Airport. In DC, we did not deplane directly into the terminal. For some reason, they had us walk downstairs onto the tarmac and then to the gate. I will never forget that deplaning process. When I got to the exit door and took my first step down onto the stairs, I looked at the grounds crew. EVERY SINGLE PERSON looked like me. There was not a White person to be seen anywhere, other than the White people who had been on our plane. Literally, every baggage person, every flight attendant— everyone I could see in every direction looked like me.

I froze on the stairs, absolutely paralyzed by the scene in front of me.

"Erin, are you ok?" My dad called to me from the ground, thinking maybe I had a leg cramp or had sprained an ankle.

"Dad, why did you never tell me there were so many people who looked like me in America?"

I can still picture the look on my father's face. He had been to DC before. He had never considered what it must feel like for me to see so many people who looked like me, to realize I was not alone.

"Honey, I'm so sorry. I just never thought about it."

I burst into tears, right there on the stairs. My father came running back to the plane to gather me in his arms. He held me there, on the tarmac, as everyone from the plane rushed by us to get their luggage.

I was overwhelmed by a sense I had not experienced before, by a knowledge that I had felt alone for all this time but had not been aware I was missing something.

Dad and I made our way to baggage claim, where the other students from the group were already waiting with their luggage. We picked up our bags and walked outside to find the bus that would take us to the hotel, where we would share rooms with students from other schools.

When we arrived at the hotel, my father asked us to stay on the bus until he connected with the program directors to make sure our paperwork was in order. My dad is a math teacher. He likes to have EVERY duck in a row before he makes any moves.

After about ten minutes, my dad re-emerged from the hotel, a giant smile on his face. He asked the students to gather their things, get off the bus and proceed to the large ballroom, where they would meet their roommates and then head to their rooms to drop off luggage before heading to opening sessions. He held me back on the bus, "Erin, you are not going to believe this! One of the partner high schools here is an all-Black school from South Carolina! You are going to be rooming with students from that school!"

I was so excited! I had found my people!

My new roommates were already in the hotel room by the time we got there. I am not usually an excitable person, but I was so excited to meet them, I could not contain myself. I opened the door to our room, put down my suitcases, and walked over to one of the girls, hand out in front of me, ready to shake, "Hi! My name is Erin. I am from The American School of The Hague."

Both girls looked at me like I had five heads and was from outer space.

"Where you from? You surely ain't from here!"

"I am from The Netherlands."

That did not help. They looked at each other, just as bewildered.

"The what...?"

"The Netherlands? It's a small country next to Germany in Europe."

"Ooooh..." her voice trailed off, a look of confusion still on her face.

I know now that she had probably never heard of The Netherlands, and she had likely never met anyone who looked like me from another country.

To make a long story short, the students from that school took me under their wings that week. They took me shopping for "Black girl clothes," and they helped me do my hair. My favorite part of the adventure was being taught their favorite dances, one of them being the Electric Slide, which remains my favorite to this day. I felt like a completely new person by the end of that week. These students could have shunned me because I was so different, but instead, they made me part of their family.

Can you remember an experience in your life where you felt a special connection with a new group of people? Have you been that connector for someone new, maybe to your school, neighborhood, or church? My week in DC was over as soon as it had begun, and the other Black students were gone. As quickly as I had found family, they were ripped away from me.

I cried as their bus drove away early Saturday morning, and I had to face the reality that snail mail (our only means of connection in the 1980s) was not enough to maintain a relationship. I knew when they drove away that day I was losing something substantial.

(Crazy fun fact: I was invited to speak at a librarians conference in 2015 in South Carolina. After my keynote, I was invited to the local all-Black high school to share my story in an all-school assembly, which we discovered was the same school that had attended CU in DC with me all those years before).

We spent the next week in Harlem visiting all the important sites there. It was such a great experience to be surrounded by Black people, see the different hairstyles and fashion, and attend a performance at the famous Apollo Theater. I could not have imagined anything so beautiful just weeks before.

I cried the entire flight home to The Netherlands after the second week. I was absolutely inconsolable. My poor dad sat next to me and tried to comfort me, but there was nothing he could do. I am sure he felt at that moment he and my mother had failed me in adopting me and raising me in Europe, away from those who looked like me. But, in all fairness, he and my mother were from Northern Minnesota. They had never lived anywhere near Black people and could not have known the impact for me of always being "the only."

When we landed in Amsterdam, my mother was there waiting for us. My mother had been my best friend since I could remember. We had always been close, partly because most of the students in our school community only stayed there for one or two years. I had learned not to bond with people I knew were going to leave me. Mom was always around. We read the same books. If I went to the movies, I usually went with her. If I went shopping for clothes or got my hair done, I went with her.

As we walked off the plane, I realized for the first time maybe my mother was not enough. Maybe she was no longer going to be able to understand me.

I could tell Mom was excited to see me and wanted to hear all about my trip, but I had no idea how to tell her about all that I had experienced. I did not know how to tell her how worried I was that maybe she was no longer enough for me. I hugged her and told her I was exhausted. I pretended to fall asleep in the back seat on our forty-five-minute drive home.

When we arrived at the house, I carried my luggage up to my room and told my parents I wanted to go straight to bed.

I cried myself to sleep that night and for the next two nights. I had left something back there in the United States. A piece of myself had not returned to The Netherlands, but I was fifteen years old and did not know how to explain what I was feeling.

Friday afternoon, just a week after our return from the United States, my parents announced they would be leaving me home alone for the weekend.

I had never stayed at home by myself—not for hours, definitely not for days.

Were they going to get a divorce? Were they headed off for crisis counseling or something?

I did not dare ask because, in my family, we did not talk about personal stuff. I was still in a sad, depressed state. I did not plan to go anywhere while they were gone. I had been coming home from school every day and going to my room to lie down and cry. I had lost something substantial, and I was not sure what to do to make things better.

Sunday evening, as I lay in my bed in the dark, I heard the front door open. My parents were home. I did not get up to greet them. The world was too heavy. I had begun to wonder if I belonged anywhere.

Suddenly there was a knock on my door, and then she opened it. Mom came into my room with a box in her hands. She put the box next to where I lay in the bed and said, "Honey, we should have done this for you a long time ago. I'm so sorry."

My parents had driven to every American bookstore in Western Europe over the weekend to buy me books about Black people, by

Black people, and for Black people. There were history books and novels and a video series called "Eyes on the Prize."

"I will read every book and watch every video with you." She paused, tears welling up in her eyes, "And I know now that someday you are going to leave us and go back to America."

For the first time, I was able to cry out loud. We cried together, holding one another in my bed. She knew what I knew—that I would inevitably return to the United States to be among people who looked like me. That realization was heavy, but I had another, more critical, realization that night—my mother was enough. She was exactly the mother I had needed all along (Love you, Mom!).

My mother and I did read the books together. We cried as we saw pictures in the history books of lynchings and beatings. We could not read through Alice Walker and Zora Neal Hurston fast enough. We watched "Eyes on the Prize" as a family.

What are the stories and histories you learned from your family? What are the stories you are telling your children or will say to them? I have often wondered how things would be different in the United States if every Black family and White family and Native family was exposed to a more complete history of the United States of America. What if the popular children's books were filled with celebrations of the wonders of indigenous cultures and the beauty of Korean art, and the wonders of Ethiopian food? What if we knew the stories of current Native leaders and more contemporary immigration stories?

As I entered junior year, I got a new AP English teacher. Ms. Nicastro was tough, but she also cared about me. Several months into the year, she approached me with several books. She thought I might enjoy reading Langston Hughes and Nella Larson from the Harlem Renaissance. I devoured the books, and she gave me more. I read James Baldwin and Maya Angelou. I read, and we discussed. Even though the stories within were different from anything I had experienced, I felt a soul-level connection to the experiences of these authors, to the cadence of their writing styles, the rhythms of their poetry.

As much as I learned about the history and literature of people who looked like me during that time, I was not prepared for the shock that would await me when I returned to the United States for college. Knowing about a people and American history is not the same as knowing a people or living in America. I was about to realize that how others perceive you and the identities you carry is almost as important as how you see yourself. I try to tell students now that they MUST control their own narratives because there are plenty of people who will try to tell your story for you in ways that are harmful if you are not in control of your own story.

The last thirty-one years in America have been a constant learning process. I met a Black man while in college, who, like me, had been exposed to music and literature and family from a variety of backgrounds. He and I had a shared love for athletics and academics. We married just months after my graduation from college.

Over time, what I have come to realize about my identity—my race, the blend of cultures I embrace, my gender, the age I am and the age people believe me to be (always significantly younger than my actual age)—is that I will never fit neatly into any boxes. I will never be Black enough for some, and I will be too Black for others. I will never be Christian enough for some, and I will be too Christian for others. I will never be liberal enough for some, and I will be too liberal for others. However, the older I get, here is what I know to be true about myself—I will always be Erin enough.

I have realized the gift that is the complexity of my identity. What I saw as a struggle—having to navigate in spaces that made me think about who I was and who I wanted to be; how I fit and how I did not—has allowed me to serve more and different people better. The diversity of places I lived, the people I met, and the literature I read have given me such a breadth of perspective that I can find connections in almost every room. I may not be able to empathize with every experience, but I have a taste of so many struggles and successes that I can think of ways to meet the differing needs of people in my space. Even now, I continue to cultivate relationships, seek out experiences that stretch me and challenge me to think outside the box and expand my thinking. I challenge myself every day to get curious, especially about those with different beliefs and experiences from my own.

The more I get to be in circles with and in proximity to those closest to the decision-making processes, the more I realize they are often making decisions based on systems that worked for them and their children. With few exceptions, these decision-makers are amazing people who work hard to read the research and look at data about trends in education. Unfortunately, however, they usually do not have skin in the game. When it comes to doing the hard things, there just is not the political will—especially when there is significant push-back from affluent members of their communities or when it comes to investing resources into programs, supports, and shifts in practice.

In the state of Washington, I watched this lack of political will result in a suit filed against the state government called The McCleary Case. I had the good fortune (hear the sarcasm in my voice) to "represent education" (yes, all of the systems of public education) during the process. My friend, a state lawmaker, serving on the Education Committee for the State Legislature, joined me in that process. In the end, the state of Washington was charged by the Supreme Court with not "amply" funding public education and being mandated to do so.

Walking through that process and living concurrently, through my own experiences with my children, I became highly aware that if anything significant was going to change, those who were genuinely interested in doing equity work would have to do their work first. They would have to unpack their own identities and realize their identities, particularly race and gender, and socioeconomic background, have huge implications for how they "get" to move through the world. Their identities are the ones that have always been centered and served in the larger systems of this country.

The most important person in the work you decide to do related to equity is you. I want to encourage you to do your own "unpacking." How has your racial identity affected how you have moved through the world? When did you first become aware of your race? Is race something you considered as you moved through your education? Is it something you thought about as you entered the world of work?

I hope that reading my story will cause you to think about your own personal journey and the ways you struggled with identity at times. Maybe your struggle with identity had more to do with gender or socioeconomic status. Use that to build a bridge to understand the struggles others have with different identities. Maybe your identities have worked for you your whole life. Perhaps this is the first time you have even considered these perspectives. That is ok. I would recommend that you get curious about others who walk in different realities as you move forward. You will have to work harder to develop the empathy necessary to move this work in the right direction.

If each one of us could get comfortable starting with ourselves, acknowledging the good, the bad, and the ugly, the ways we have benefitted from systems and practices or been marginalized we could do the work necessary to move us into a better version of ourselves (as individual people, schools, businesses, agencies, a nation. We cannot fix what we are not willing to face.

# 9

# IMPLICATIONS FOR YOUR PERSONAL STORY

The last chapter was primarily devoted to sharing my personal story, particularly the ways race informed how I moved through the world as a child and then as an adult. Each of our stories will be different. How White people understand their own racial identities (or do not, because often White people do not think they have a racial identity) is very different. I hope to help you think about your own stories and the implications for how you came to understand your stories, whether you would be raced as White or as Black, Brown or Native.

I want to begin with an experience I had with my mother, who would be raced as White and raised in a small Iron Range town of Northern Minnesota, a town created several generations ago for the Finnish immigrants. They were not welcome in the larger neighboring town, Grand Rapids, where my father, of Norwegian heritage, grew up.

As I shared in my personal story, my parents adopted me and then left the United States to raise me in the Netherlands. We did not talk about race at all until I was in the tenth grade after my trip to Washington, DC, and Harlem. My parents realized they had not done the work of helping me understand my ethnic heritage, the history of "my people" in the United States.

Although my mother spent dozens of hours with me from sophomore year to senior year reading books and watching videos about Black people, and we learned a ton about the Black experience in the United States, neither of us realized until almost two decades later that her identity as a White woman (not just as a Scandinavian-American) mattered as much as my identity as a woman raced as Black.

My mother loved to make the Norwegian Christmas cookies of my father's tradition. She even made lefse on occasion, spread with butter. However, it was not until she and my father retired in the United States that we had to have a reckoning about the role her race played in how she moved through the world. Even though she had raised me and we shared many of the same behaviors and cultural norms, her skin color affected how people perceived and treated her.

This would all become blatantly apparent within a year of her return to the United States. She and Dad decided to retire near me to be close to my children. They had spent extended vacations near or with us during the children's elementary years, but my parents were excited to be able to now help with homework and attend both sporting and music events to play significant roles in the lives of their grandchildren.

Just over a year after my parents had moved to our community, I was promoted to the cabinet for the State Superintendent. I became one of the only women and the only Black person in the cabinet. I was also one of the only recent classroom teachers in that role, which meant there were ways I was connected to what was currently happening in public schools that others were not. One day, early in my new role, I was called down to the Superintendent's office. He had been asked to deliver the keynote address at the state superintendents' conference, but something had come up, so he could not attend. He knew I liked public speaking and offered me the opportunity to stand in on his behalf.

"Is there anything specific you want me to talk about?"

Nope. He said I could talk about anything of interest to me.

I knew immediately I would share my WHY story. I knew how important it was, especially for leaders, to be reminded why they had gotten into this profession in the first place. The work was hard. It was easy to slip into routines and lose the passion that once was a fire inside you, motivating you to go above and beyond expectations.

I was ecstatic to have this opportunity. I immediately thought of my mother. I knew she had not yet visited Yakima, and I figured this would be an excellent opportunity for a road trip. Mom was excited to attend with me.

The night before our trip, I picked out my favorite Calvin Klein suit and matching heels. I pressed my hair and wrapped it, so I would have little to do in the morning. The following morning, I drove to her home to pick her up just before dawn. She came out to the car in her favorite White no-iron blouse and tan pants. We made the three-hour trek across the mountains to the Yakima Convention Center.

We talked the entire way—about the kids, about the new bulbs she was planting in her garden, about my new role as Assistant State Superintendent. Mom was my best friend. We could talk about anything. I was so happy to have her back in my daily life. After all, I had lived in the United States without her for twenty years. This new season was such a gift.

When we arrived in the parking lot at the Convention Center, the butterflies began to dance in my stomach—I was about to do a keynote at a superintendents' conference! I still could not believe I, just a classroom teacher a year earlier, was about to address a ballroom full of superintendents!

Mom followed me into the Convention Center, which I had visited before on several occasions, for conferences I hosted on family engagement. As we entered the lobby, an older woman walked up to us and addressed my mother, "Oh, you must be Erin Jones, our keynote speaker!"

To this day, I do not know what about my mother screamed, "Assistant State Superintendent!" She was not wearing a suit. She had a purse, not a briefcase.

My mother is not one to raise her voice or visibly display anger (although I know her well enough to know when she is upset by the look in her eyes and feel of her body). I could feel her body heating up, immediately. If you have ever seen a cartoon image of a character's head opening up and fire flaming out, that is exactly what I imagined happening in my mother's body at that moment.

Before I could say anything, my mother was shouting and finger-wagging, "This is my daughter, Erin Jones, and SHE is your keynote speaker today!" She did not wait for the woman to respond, "Erin, give me your keys!" She put out her hand. I reached into my purse, pulled my keys out, and dropped them into her hand, now shaking in anger. My mother stormed out of the lobby and then outside into the early morning sun.

I was left standing there, stunned. I was not sure what had just happened or why my mother was SO angry.

Press "pause" for a moment. You may wonder how a six-foot-tall Black woman could be invisible to the conference organizer, especially considering how I dressed, in contrast to how my mother dressed. Imagine being raised in an environment where you never saw a Black or Brown woman in charge of anything. Imagine if every leader you had ever seen was always a White woman or White man and often of more advanced age. When our personal experiences have trained us to have certain expectations, our eyes will naturally begin to seek representations that match those expectations. This woman likely didn't have malicious intent towards me. She just did not have a mental model to imagine me in such a prestigious role. Her reaction was likely more a demonstration of naïveté than it was of intentional bias.

The woman in charge of the conference was equally stunned by my mother's response. She gasped for air, gulped, and then asked me to follow her into the ballroom where she had the agenda for the conference and a bottle of water. "If you would like coffee or a pastry, they are at the back of the room. Help yourself."

She never did apologize for her mistake. I do not know if she even realized what she had done. Although I would definitely take the time now to "educate" someone with a similar reaction, as a brand new executive dealing with a bit of imposter syndrome (thinking maybe I did not even deserve to be there in that capacity), I did not yet have the confidence to educate her or push back in any way.

We walked silently towards the head table, both of us likely in a bit of shock. I looked at all the people in the room. Every single person was White. Every single person was in their late fifties or older. Almost every person was male. The number of shiny, hairless heads was noticeable.

Although I had been a bit hungry, I had no appetite now. The woman led me to my seat and then said she would be back momentarily. She needed to do some additional setup for the day. I sat in my chair and picked up the conference agenda. "Rural-Remote Superintendents Conference, 2009."

Rural-remote superintendents?!

My boss had not told me I would be talking to superintendents of our schools out in the country! What did I know about those places? I had never taught in a rural-remote space. In fact, at that time, I had never even visited a rural-remote school. So what the heck could I say to these people that would resonate for them?

I sat in my seat sweating bullets. I was alone at the table. My mother was not with me. I was suddenly aware I was the youngest one in the room and the only Brown person, except for the wait staff busy cleaning empty coffee cups and plates off tables as superintendents networked with one another.

Why had I said YES to this opportunity? This was no opportunity at all! I was about to bomb this, my first big keynote address.

When the time came to speak, I decided to give the speech I had initially prepared for—my WHY education story. I hoped, even though my story would be light years different from anyone else in this room, it would cause at least some leaders to think differently about their own WHY stories and, maybe, about how they saw Black people and how they saw urban schools.

When I had said my last word, almost every person in that room jumped to their feet. There was thunderous applause. They liked my speech! I was so happy to have worn a suit. The blouse underneath was drenched in sweat. I felt like I was about to faint, but I had made it! I made my boss proud.

Pause. So often, we think we need to become "something" else to be heard. We believe we need to dress and act and speak like other people to be accepted. If anything I learned at that moment has been reinforced, it is that when we communicate out of authentic passion, the message will be heard and confirmed. People can listen to and feel "fake." I tell students all the time to show up as their full selves, even if their selves don't make them cool or popular. It is no different for adults. If we can't show up as our full selves, we cannot show up as our best selves.

I looked out over the audience to find my mother, to share this special moment with her. She was nowhere to be found.

She was not in the ballroom.

She was not in the bathroom.

She was not in the lobby.

She was nowhere in the building.

I remembered I had given her my keys. I hoped I would find her out in the car, but I could not believe she would have stayed out there all that time. I could not believe she would have missed her daughter's keynote speech.

As I neared my car, I could see my mother sitting in the passenger seat. Phew! At least she was safe. She was here. I got in the car and began to ask her if she had been here all this time. Before any words could leave my mouth, I could see she had been crying. Her face was still covered in tears.

"Mom! Are you okay? What's wrong?"

Life was about to change for both of us, in ways we could not have imagined just hours before.

"Erin, I know you have said you often feel invisible at work, that people don't see you or listen to you or take you seriously. I have never understood that. I know you are so smart, and you've won all these awards for teaching, so obviously, you are good at what you do... and you are six feet tall! How could anyone not see you..." She began to cry again. "I couldn't understand how it was possible for people not to see you until today. How did that woman not know you were the keynote speaker? *You* are the Assistant Superintendent, not me!"

Now we were both crying. My mother does not show this kind of emotion often. We talk a lot about a lot, but how she feels is not one of our conversation topics.

"Erin, I guess the thing I realized today... and it's why I couldn't come back inside. I realized now that probably most of the men you work with don't actually have any Black friends. They probably don't even know any Black people and aren't around any, unless they are being served in a restaurant or something... so, of course they don't actually SEE you." She took another deep breath. "The most important thing I realized today, though, is that maybe I wouldn't see you, either, if you were not my daughter."

*What?!*

Maybe I wouldn't see you either if you were not my daughter.

Sit with that for a moment. Who are the "invisible" people in your world, the people you do not hate or even dislike but do not have any experience or familiarity and may pass right by them without any engagement? Those experiencing homelessness? Those who speak a language with which you are unfamiliar?

"Honey, if you were not my daughter, maybe I would see all Black people like they do. Maybe I would be just like them."

Right there, in the car, everything changed.

My mother and I held each other, and we cried.

My mother had known all this time that we were different, but it was not until that moment, that encounter with a White person who did not see me as possibly being the "special guest," that my mother had a realization of the work she needed to do, of her own privilege.

Ever since that day, my mother has been a different person. My mother has paid attention in new ways to how I am treated in stores and in restaurants and how she is treated differently. She has watched the ways my children are treated—where they are expected to be brilliant (music) and where they are doubted (academics). It has pained her greatly knowing she cannot protect us, knowing that our skin color makes us "dangerous" or "not smart enough," and she has had to wrestle with what that means for her and how she can advocate on our behalf and empathize in new ways when she hears the many stories I tell.

For those of you who are raced as White and do not have an adopted Black daughter or Asian son or Native American son or Latina daughter or spouse or partner, you may wonder if you will ever be able to empathize with the experience my mother had or truly know the experience of your non-White neighbors or colleagues. Choose to make a connection. Now, I do not suggest you adopt a child or start dating a person of color. I do have a suggestion, though, in the form of another story I hope will help you understand how you can play a different role in developing the relationships you need to embrace this work in a personal way truly. There are ways you can choose to show up for and care for people who you do not often see or know intimately.

My formative years as an athlete were in a unique context— American and international schools competing against one another across Western Europe. We began traveling out of the country for sporting events when I was ten years old. Now, I should mention that it takes about the same amount of time to drive from The Hague, The Netherlands, to Düsseldorf, Germany, as it takes from Olympia, Washington to Portland, Oregon. The trip out of the country sounds much more exciting, but when you are on a bus with dozens of pre-teens, the smell is pretty much the same.

Our team from the American School of The Hague typically drove to a place, played a game, and then stayed in the home of one of our opponents for the evening so that we could play another game the next day. Although most students at international schools in Europe only stayed for two to three years (the average tour of duty for most in the military or serving as executives for international companies), those of us who stuck around for years developed strong bonds to families of other players our age. Many of us played more than one sport, so we would stay with a family not just once a year but sometimes multiple times. As a result, those families got to know us. We saw one another as opponents, yes, but we were also friends.

My father came to most of my games, but he could not get out of school in enough time when those games were more than four hours away. He did not ever fly to England for our matches against the American School of London or the Community School of Surrey. It was not his voice cheering me on in the stands for those games. I clearly remember the mother or father of my "houser" (that is what we called the people in whose houses we stayed for the evening) cheering for me when I hit a home run in a softball game or made a great play on the basketball court. I distinctly remember the mother of my houser running out on the court when I got knocked down, and she thought I had sprained my ankle. I may not have been her daughter, but she had built enough of a connection with me that I was not just some anonymous player.

What does this have to do with our conversations about race, equity, and justice?

It has been my experience that White people who do racial

equity work are either like my mother—people who have a vested stake in the ground because of a very intimate personal relationship —or they are like the mom of the girl on the "other" team. White people who stay in the work stay engaged because they are already bonded in a relationship with someone who is personally impacted. They CHOOSE to bind themselves to a person or to a group of people they see is impacted.

Staying committed to equity work requires seeing yourself invested in more than just what is good for yourself and your family. That is true for those of us who identify as non-White as well. Commitment to equity requires seeing your flourishing as bound to the flourishing of others around you who may need cheerleaders on occasion or medics or coaches or referees. Where do opportunities exist for you to build relationships with those who are different from you? Are there organizations like the NAACP or Centro Latino or a Korean Women's Association with events you could attend to begin building personal relationships that drive you to greater compassion and concern for those who may be experiencing your community in very different ways?

As for those of us who are raced as Black, Asian, Latinx, and Native, we have our own work to do. There is a dynamic at play in the United States of one group fighting against another for scraps, instead of focusing on similar ways groups experience marginalization or oppression and advocating together to ensure greater thriving. Different ethnic groups tend to fight against one another for opportunities and resources. In my imagined "healthy" world, I see us all linked together, across races, doing whatever is necessary to ensure systems and practices and ways of being are in place that enables all of us to thrive, no matter our color or gender, or religious practice or geographic location.

Additionally, we need to be mindful of the ways systems will fight to maintain the status quo. Change is hard and uncomfortable. Many will pressure us to keep things as they are, not to challenge what is currently in play, because it works for them. Some of the tactics to watch out for are perfection and defensiveness. There will be those who become paralyzed because they do not have the perfect equity statement or do not know the exact "right" way to respond to a situation. Others will take even the conversation about race as a personal attack, "Just talking about race is racist."

These responses often do not come from a place of malice but of ignorance and naïveté. We hate to have our flaws pointed out, especially when we do not have the correct responses or are unaware of appropriate actions. We hate to think that we are being accused of being "bad" people because we say or do the wrong thing.

Resist the urge to succumb to these strategies. If we are going to be and to build bridges that heal US as a nation, it will require fighting against the habits we have developed that encourage us not to have hard conversations, that enable us to get defensive when someone critiques us (and then to stop engaging), that cause us to think we can and should do everything on our own, that we ourselves are enough, that we do not need to hear the voices of others with different experiences and perspectives. We absolutely can accomplish this task, but not without effort, discomfort, and accountability to and from others to which we see ourselves bound.

We can if we choose.

I invite you to let your identity BE a bridge for others to cross when appropriate or necessary. I invite you to let your identities help you BUILD bridges for others to join you on the journey. When necessary, be willing to cross the BRIDGES others have built when you do not have the strength to BE or BUILD yourself. The work is big enough and heavy enough to require all of us to be involved in whatever way possible to move to our healing.

# 10

# UNDERSTANDING OTHER

There are stories we tell and are told about whole swaths of people in the United States. These stories live in the back of our heads and will come flooding forward in moments of intense emotion or frustration, or anger. The stories themselves do not make us "good" or "bad" people. They make us human. We have to work hard to unpack those stories, face them, and replace them with new ones. I have had to (and continue to) face the stories I have consumed and embraced through my lifetime.

About seventeen years ago, while teaching French Immersion for Tacoma Public Schools, I was invited by a friend to meet the person at our state department of education who was doing work to better support students of color in public education. This gentleman was getting ready to deliver a workshop to educators and wanted to partner with an up-and-coming classroom teacher to make sure the instruction was delivered in a way that would be relevant to current practitioners.

We met for coffee and talked about what he hoped to accomplish in the training. At the time, I had never delivered professional development beyond my school building. I was still of the mind that I would stay in the classroom working with children forever. I remember listening to this state administrator lay out his plan for the training, thinking, "Something is missing. The information is important, but it is going to go in one ear and out the other."

That is when I had an idea. I really do not know where the idea came from. I had never seen anyone do this. I guess I had spent so much time at that point creating lessons and developing ideas on my own for my French Immersion students that involved theater and music and art, and my brain was wide open to lots of ideas.

"I hear you say you want to talk about the different stereotypes we as a country have about different races, but what if you didn't just list them out? What if we role-played and had people SEE the ways we stereotype people?"

He looked confused. In my mind, I could see a vision that I was struggling to communicate.

"What if I were to dress up like a basketball player and come into the session. And you ask the participants what they see when they see me? Like, how old do you think she is? Where do you think she is from? What do you think her dreams are? What do you think she is good at? What if you were to ask those questions after I left the room, and then I could come back in with my suit on, and they could get the actual answers? From me?"

At first, the two gentlemen who had invited me to meet about training were not so sure about this idea. It definitely was not a traditional approach to training. I explained to them it might be more potent for people to have a physical and emotional experience regarding the effects of stereotyping than if we were to merely talk about typical stereotypes.

Training day came. The room was filled with teachers. The gentlemen began the training, introducing themselves and providing an overview of the session they were about to provide, devoted to a discussion of the power and danger of stereotypes in our practice as teachers. They said they had a special guest they wanted to introduce to the group.

I came into the room. The men asked their questions of the

participants. Not one person got a question correct. I returned to the room minutes later dressed "like a teacher."

Although I am well-known in education circles now, at the time, I was "no one." People had bought hook, line, and sinker into the stereotypes we had fed them. They were absolutely blown away once they knew the truth—that the woman they thought was a teen basketball star was actually a teacher, like them, who could also speak four languages and had traveled to fourteen countries, who had been educated at one of the best elite private colleges in the country.

Once we had unpacked the "truth" about my story, we talked about the many ways teachers stereotype students and, thus, limit their potential. We talked about the importance of disrupting narratives and challenging the stories we have been told about different groups of people, particularly students of color.

I would go on to do similar presentations for over a decade following that experiment. People who attended those events—sometimes in large auditoriums; at times in small classrooms—still talk about those presentations today. They talk about the emotions elicited by that experience and how it caused them to reimagine the potential of the students who sit in their classrooms every year.

The truth is that all of us are affected by the stories we have been exposed to on television, in the news, in textbooks, and from our families. Anyone who has lived in the United States for more than a year has heard and seen powerful, negative images of Black, Brown, and Native people. In truth, it does not take a person being "bad" to believe these stories or to continue to perpetuate them in the ways we interact.

Every nation has its "single stories" beyond those related to race. In the Netherlands, where I spent my formative years, there were stories told about "all Germans" in response to World War II atrocities. Even though not every German fought on behalf of the Nazis or supported their cause, to the Dutch people who lost so much in the war, EVERY German was bad. As a child, I watched

Dutch people egg cars with German license plates during the Europa Cup in The Netherlands.

I had so many friends from Germany because of my many travels as a student-athlete that, although I grieved what the Dutch had lost during World War II, I also did not hold EVERY German responsible for the atrocities that took place there.

I will acknowledge that there were powerful stereotypes I had to overcome. Although I did not have many experiences with Black people while living in Europe, it did not take long living in the United States, in a very wealthy suburb of Philadelphia, to develop ideas about "those Black people" who lived in the city (or "the hood," as many referred to it). I quickly developed ideas about "appropriate" dress for Black males (which did not include sagging pants or unlaced shoes). I quickly internalized the notion that Black males who dressed "that way" were up to no good and were likely in gangs.

At the beginning of my junior year of college, a Barnes and Nobles bookstore appeared in our college town. As a lover of books, I had to see this bookstore that was rumored to have more than one floor and comfortable chairs to sit and read in (like a library). When I entered the store for the first time, I was drawn to the beautiful wood staircase leading to a second floor. I did not know what was upstairs, but the staircase was so beautiful, I had to go check it out. As soon as I stepped onto the last stair, what caught my attention immediately was the woman who was in charge of the children's section. She was Black, and she was the most beautiful woman I had seen.

Black people did not work in visible positions in Bryn Mawr. If you were Black, you were relegated to the kitchen, janitorial staff, or bussing tables. There were no Black cashiers or waiters.

This Black woman was the only person upstairs, and she had a name tag on with Barnes and Nobles etched into it. She was official. "Excuse me."

She looked up. I do not know who was more surprised and excited to see whom.

Her name was Sheila Drapiewski. She was, indeed, in charge of the children's section three afternoons each week. She was a third-grade special education teacher in Philadelphia. Her school did not have money to buy her children books, so she drove over an hour from her home to work in this store three days a week and worked five hours each day, on top of her full-time teaching schedule. She used her salary and employee discount to buy books for her classroom.

I wanted to BE this woman.

On that first encounter, I asked Mrs. Drapiewski if she needed any volunteers. Was there a way I could help out in her classroom? I knew instinctively I needed to learn from this woman. There was something magical about her—her clarity of purpose, her love of students, her commitment.

I started volunteering with Mrs. Drapiewski twice a week in the off-season (basketball season did not allow for me to make the trek two hours each way). I remember the first time I visited her school. I had to take a trolley to the El and then to a bus. The bus dropped me off in one of the most desolate spots in North Philadelphia. To this day, I do not remember how I got past the group of gang leaders standing on the corner openly brandishing their weapons.

The police did not engage in that community at the time, as I would later learn, which is what allowed these men free reign. There was a bullet out on the street called "the cop killer." The bullet was made to go through bulletproof vests. Instead of creating stronger armor, the police just removed themselves from the neighborhood.

I can honestly say I judged every person I walked by in that neighborhood for the first week. The men all had sagging pants and wore rags either on their heads or in their pockets or wrapped around a wrist. I assumed every last one of them was up to no good... was, in fact, no good.

As much as 80% of the students in that school lived in homes that had been boarded up and forcefully vacated for any number of reasons. These students lived without running water or electricity. For most of them, the only food they received was the food they could get for breakfast and then for lunch at school. The children typically had one outfit they wore every day, an outfit that was often covered in whatever they had eaten over the last week or with the dirt from dust that covered floors and walls in homes that had no electricity for a vacuum.

I will never forget one of my first days in Mrs. Drapiewski's classroom. A little boy refused to enter the class at the beginning of the day. He stood at the door, angry and then in tears. He had soiled his pants in the middle of the night and was embarrassed to have to expose himself to his classmates. Sheila had a solution. She had a storage closet in the hall in which she stored clean clothing in various sizes for just such an occasion. She asked me to stay in the classroom while she got the little boy cleaned up and in a new outfit for the day. She informed me that there was a washer and dryer down the hall for these occasions and let me know she had a policy to always send the children back in the clothes they had shown up to school in or parents would become angry (poverty does not erase pride). When the little boy returned to class with Mrs. Drapiewski, she thanked me for supervising the class and asked if I would sit with him at the back of the room for a bit and read him stories until he was able to calm himself.

I was happy to oblige. I love to read books out loud, and I felt honored to serve in this way. The little boy came back to the table and sat next to me, so close his little body was pressed against mine. He trembled a bit, still trying to recover from his crying fit. I read him a book and then began another. After about ten minutes, Sheila called over, "Ok. Time to get back to class, Jared."

"Just one more book, Mrs. Drapiewski, please?"

"I don't mind reading one more, if that helps."

What was about to come out of her mouth would change my life and forever inform how I teach.

"Erin, compassion says we give him a clean outfit and help him get calm, but then it's time to learn. Our pity is not useful. Our pity is not going to help him get out of this situation. He NEEDS to learn to read and write and do math, so his family is not stuck like this. He needs our compassion. He doesn't need our pity."

Her words struck home. I am reminded of a phrase, apparently made famous by George W. Bush in 2000 in a speech to the NAACP, where he spoke of "the soft bigotry of low expectations."

Sheila knew she needed to have high expectations for students, but she also provided them with high levels of support. She modeled that every day. Another phrase of hers I will never forget was, "Erin, one of these students may have the cure for cancer. I don't know which one it will be, but I am going to teach each one as if they might be the one who has the cure inside them."

Wow!

She completely changed how I thought about poor people and, in particular, poor Black people. I learned through a Google search in the process of writing this book that Sheila Drapievski recently retired from a career as a principal in Philadelphia Public Schools. I am not at all surprised.

I did not earn my teaching certificate at Bryn Mawr because there was no teacher education program, but I was still committed to working with students. My husband and I were married in South Bend, so I started my teaching career there as a long-term substitute at Clay Middle School. Although I enjoyed my time at Clay, the money was not much. We struggled to pay bills.

One day while playing basketball with a bunch of local PE teachers and athletic coaches, I was invited to apply to teach at a private school—The Stanley Clark School. I taught seventh grade English and PE. There were only five Black students in the school at the time, and all were on scholarship. The one Black boy in my grade struggled to turn in homework. I became more and more concerned. It did not matter what notes I sent home with him. His work was not getting done. My husband offered to drive with me to visit his home. He still talks about the visit to this day, particularly now that he is a teacher. We discovered quickly why this young man was not doing homework. He was not the only child in his home, and there was no quiet place to do work. There was not even a kitchen table or other surface upon which he could have done his homework.

I had assumed this young man just did not care enough about his schoolwork, that he was not dedicated enough. That was not the case at all. He just did not have the structures or resources in place to be able to do what he needed to be successful. I asked his mother if he could either come to school early or stay late. I was willing to add extra time to my schedule to ensure he was able to demonstrate the brilliance I knew was inside of him.

He found his way, and I learned to be better for him and others, not make assumptions about why students were not showing up in the ways I expected, and always ask WHY.

Who are the "others" for you? Who are the groups of students or the neighborhoods for which you have a "single story" that shapes (negatively) how you think about them?

If you are a teacher, maybe a White boy "acts up," and you write it off as "boys will be boys," but a Black or Latino boy does the same thing, and they are suddenly a "problem."

Maybe you are a White male business owner and, in the process of doing interviews, you notice an Asian or Native American applicant never looks anyone on your team in the eye, and you assume it is because they do not know how to show respect, instead of recognizing that respect is demonstrated differently by different ethnic groups.

Maybe you are a neighbor, and you notice a family seems to leave their children home a lot on their own, unsupervised. You are not sure how old the children are, but you were raised to believe that children should not be left alone until they are teenagers. So you write that family off as uncaring or irresponsible when, in fact, the children are all middle-school-aged, and both mother and father are working multiple jobs to pay the bills.

We each make assumptions about people without having all the information. What if we got curious about those who look different or act differently instead of getting judgmental? Instead of jumping to conclusions about whole groups of people, why not start asking questions and, at least, do some Google research.

Who are you following on social media? Does everyone in your feed look like you and share similar beliefs and experiences? That is probably a good sign you need to diversify your friend circle. Get intentional. Start by following a famous person you respect. Please pay attention to what they post, what seems to matter most to them.

What are the movies and television shows you are watching? What are the narratives those shows are promoting? Which types of characters are presented as good and successful, and who is bad? Who is altogether absent?

Do you have thirty minutes each week you could devote to volunteering for an organization that serves a community with which you are not familiar? Could you show up consistently for a few months to serve others, learn about their needs (by watching and listening to them), and create connections. You never know what those few months could do to change your outlook on your own experience and, therefore, on the world, and what more expansive thriving could look like.

Although truly interrogating systems requires more study into history and policy, this process in your community is a critical beginning to understanding what equity could look like in your context.

# 11

# INTERROGATING SYSTEMS

In the last several years, I have seen a pattern of rhetoric proclaiming there is no relevance to conversations about race and systems. Race plays no role in informing how systems work differently for Black, Brown, and Native people. There are many who, when they see the words "systems" and "race" together, respond with, "Oh, but slavery ended so long ago. Since that time, law and policy have been blind to race."

Unfortunately, this kind of response uncovers our lack of knowledge of history as a nation. So many people are completely unaware of Jim Crow laws which outlined where people of African descent could eat and swim and use the restroom. Although these laws existed primarily in the South, there were northern states with Jim-Crow-like laws that dictated where people of African descent could live and what was required for a person of African descent to vote. Many are unaware of the Native American boarding schools where scores of indigenous children were forced to attend, stripped of their Native customs and languages up until, in some places, as late as the late 70s. Many are unaware of the internment of Japanese people in camps, like the one at the Washington State Fairgrounds, during the Second World War. These people had often been born in the United States and had American citizenship, but they still had their land and businesses taken away and interred in camps. Not to mention the practice of redlining that forced Black and Brown people into the poorest and most under-resourced communities in a metropolitan area up until the 80s in some regions. All of these realities have implications today for how families were removed from opportunities to build wealth or access health care or high-quality education.

This lack of historical knowledge is at times innocent and at other times intentional. School districts in the South intentionally forbade teachers from teaching about the evils of slavery and insisted only positive stories be told. There are districts across the nation today that forbid any teaching of ethnic studies or mentions of the damages done by White people or the treaties that were broken between the American government and indigenous people. More common is a practice of teaching the same stories we heard as youth, stories that maintain the status quo, stories that present White males as the heroes.

This gap in knowledge, for whatever reason, is particularly dangerous because of the ways it affects how decision-makers understand the world and how they and others move through it. I have spent over a decade working with and around decision-makers —from elected officials to state executives to school district super-intendents to business owners. I have also provided training for staff of these decision-makers and members of churches and non-profit organizations and students at every level of education. I have seen a common theme across these two sectors as we talk about race and equity. Leaders know Black and Brown and Native people are experiencing harm as they engage systems, but they are unfamiliar with the history of those systems. Decision-makers often want to jump immediately to writing new policies and interrupting patterns of harm at the systems level without doing the personal work or build the relationships with marginalized communities that are required actually to know what necessary, effective change might look like. Individuals want to focus only on interpersonal interactions and often do not see their role in informing systems and policy. My greatest passion in this work is to get both groups to do it all—to better understand who they are and how they move in systems, to engage and build relationships with those in their communities who are different from them, and then to leverage that new knowledge to push for legislative and systemic change that leads to flourishing.

Although leaders typically have a better-than-average understanding of the role of systems in how people access wealth and well-being, I have also come to believe that far too many leaders do not see the ways race influences how systems work in the world. The same is true for the average person on the street. They know it is bad to call someone a name, but they do not see the other insidious ways people with brown skin tones are treated differently by the systems we all interact with daily.

I want to share a story about my oldest son that demonstrates the multiple ways we must engage on the subject of racial equity if we hope to see any meaningful change.

Our family moved to a small town just north of Spokane, Washington, in 2006. For those who are not familiar with Washington State, Spokane is a predominantly White city on the eastern side of the state. Although there are several Native tribes in the area, there are not substantial numbers of Black or Brown people in the area. We moved to Spokane for several reasons. I had been working with a group of students of color from the Tacoma area who were preparing to attend Whitworth University, a predominantly White, private, Christian liberal arts college in Spokane. I was offered a job supporting those students on campus, although the job fell through at the last minute due to a budget cut. We decided to move, anyway. Our niece had just lost her mother to an overdose and needed a fresh start. The timing seemed right.

As we prepared for the move, we shared stories with our children about the numerous visits my husband and I had made to

Spokane to visit the university, to do church missions trips. We warned them that they would likely be some of the only non-White children in their school. We invited them not to take any ignorant comments personally and to assume other children just had no experience with kids who looked like them.

Minutes into the first day of school, our niece (now our adopted daughter) called me at work, "Auntie Erin, you lied to us!"

What? (I did not make a practice of lying to my children.)

"You told us we would be 'some of the only' kids of color in our school. We are the *only* ones here!"

She was angry.

"I am so sorry, honey. I really thought there would at least be a few more. Honey, I know it's hard to look different from other kids, but just be you. You will make friends."

She did. She is my most social kid. She was fine.

Our youngest son was accepted into the gifted program and would be bussed away to a special location two days a week to do school with other children who loved to read and do science. School seemed to work well for him.

My oldest son had been diagnosed with dysgraphia just two years prior and was served by a 504 Plan, a legal document that was meant to ensure he received support for writing and organization. His brain and his hand do not talk to one another. He is unable to think linearly. If he does not connect to what you are saying, he will find something else of greater interest. He just might start singing. (It's funny and very true, even today).

We attended all the parent nights available. We introduced ourselves to all the teachers. People knew I was an instructional coach at a high school in the city and that my husband worked with students through a local non-profit. Everything seemed to be going well, and then, in the first week of December, I received a call from our oldest son's teacher, "Mrs. Jones, Malachi has not turned in any assignments for the last month. This is a problem."

A month? And you are just now telling me?

"I wish you had let me know much sooner."

"Mrs. Jones, I have been sick and have not been in school. Now that I am back, I will make sure I stay on top of things."

"Malachi does homework every night. I will take some time to look in his backpack tonight. If you would be willing tomorrow to have him clean out his desk, I bet most of the assignments are there. I work with him every night. And, if you don't mind (I know this is already in his 504 Plan), could you check in with him first thing each day and ask him for his homework? Otherwise, he will not remember to turn it in."

She promised to support us in this way. We went through his backpack at home that evening. I discovered many completed assignments shoved into the far reaches of his backpack. We unfolded them, put them under large textbooks to flatten out overnight, and I sent him to school the next day with all of his work in a file folder, with instructions to turn the entire folder into his teacher as soon as he got to school.

We did not receive another call. I continued to sit with Malachi every night as he completed his homework. I assumed things were fine. Winter Break came and went.

School resumed in January. Just before the end of semester, I received another call, "Mrs. Jones, if Malachi doesn't start turning in his work, he is likely going to have to repeat the fifth grade."

"Wait! Have you not been getting his homework each morning?"

"No, Mrs. Jones. I have still not received anything from him."

Wait. Nothing? Since December?

"Have you been asking him each morning to give you his home-work folder, as we discussed the last time we talked."

"No, Mrs. Jones. He is in fifth grade now. He needs to remember to turn that in himself."

Ok... We had talked. She had made a promise. I had the legal documentation of his 504 Plan that required special accommodations. I was only asking for this small accommodation. I am a teacher. I knew how this worked.

I was not happy.

I left my school early and drove out to his school, arriving just as the last bell rang. I told the other two children to take the bus home and asked Malachi to stay behind. We needed to visit his teacher.

She was not excited to see me.

I opened Malachi's backpack. There was his folder with the day's homework still inside. I asked him to show me his desk. Even from a distance I could see dozens of papers shoved inside. I knew I would find each one of his homework assignments there.

There were at least six weeks of assignments shoved at all angles into his small desk. I pulled each one out and had Malachi explain to me the order in which he had completed them. We placed them in order and then in his homework folder and handed it to the teacher.

"Malachi, you know these were all due last week. Last week was the last day I took late work." She would not make eye contact with me. "You may not have credit for any of these assignments."

I was about to vomit... or scream.

I asked Malachi to wait outside and closed the door.

I explained in very gentle tones to his teacher that, although I could appreciate that she was obviously ill and not at the top of her game, this behavior was absolutely unacceptable. She had made a promise to me, which could be enforced by the legal document we had completed in the 504 Plan. How could you physically see he had completed all his assignments and still choose to give him no credit?

Although I knew I could move him to the other fifth grade teacher across the hall, I decided that day to move him to the other elementary school, which was also closer to our home. We had been sent to the school over the boundary, because our neighborhood school was overcrowded. I informed the teacher he would not be returning to her classroom. He would no longer be a burden to her.

We left the school and went home. Malachi would begin the new semester in a different school within walking distance from our home. His brother and sister would remain at their school several miles away, separated from him.

Within days of a new semester, the phone rang in my office, "Mrs. Jones, this is the principal at your Malachi's school. I don't have your husband's number, but I need to see you both immediately! It is an urgent situation."

Seriously?! We had just been through the wringer at the last school! I called my husband on his cell phone and left work early again.

We showed up at the front of the school at about the same time. I was in a suit with my official Rogers High School "instructional coach" badge on. He was business casual, having come straight from the office. We rushed into the building to the front office. The principal was waiting there. He was a little man compared to us. He almost cowered in front of us as he said, "You must be the Joneses. Please come into my office."

"Where is our son? Is he okay?"

The principal's little body trembled. His face was red. "Please follow me into my office. Let's talk in here. Please have a seat, Mr. and Mrs. Jones."

I was not about to sit down. I wanted to know where our son was. Was he okay? Was he at the hospital?

"Ma'am, please have a seat."

"I am not sitting down until I know my son is okay."

"Well..." the poor man stammered and tried to put words together for several seconds, before he finally blurted out, "Malachi was called a monkey on the playground today by another child. I have suspended that child, but I thought you should know..."

Before he could say anything more, I burst into laughter. It is not that I thought my son being called a monkey was funny. I was just prepared for so much worse.

"Mrs. Jones, this is not a joke. We take this very seriously. We don't tolerate this kind of behavior here."

"Sir, I am not laughing because I think this is funny. I really was ready for something so much worse. Where is Malachi now?"

"We sent him home about a half an hour ago. We suspended the other child, though. I want you to know that. This is not who we are here..."

LOL. "This is not who we are" in my book is code for, 'We have not yet had the opportunity to manifest who we are, because there have not yet been Black students in our midst.'

"First of all, I need you to bring that other child back to school. I am a teacher. Suspending him for calling my son a name is not going to make things better. Bring him back tomorrow, please. Second, can I ask if my son is the only Black student in your school?"

He nodded, confirmation of what I already knew to be true.

"I expect you to get that child and my son together tomorrow to talk this out." I turned to my husband, "Honey, let's go!"

Who sends a ten-year-old child home to an empty house after a traumatic event like that? Who does that?! I was beside myself.

We lived just blocks from the school and were home within minutes. Malachi was in front of our house. He did not have a key because Malachi tended to lose or misplace anything not permanently attached to his body. His backpack was on the front stoop. He was dancing in the driveway and singing at the top of his lungs.

Yes, this was the child who had just been called a "monkey," dancing and singing, completely unaware of the world around him.

Dad and I pulled into the driveway. I jumped out of the car, "Malachi, how was your day at school today?"

"I had an awesome day!"

"Really? Tell me about your day."

"Well, my new teacher is a man, and he loves to talk about sports, just like me. I really like him."

"Anything else happen today?"

"I made some new friends."

Remember I told you Malachi is dysgraphic? He also has ADD, which means things that happened in the past are way in the past, not at top of mind, non-existent.

"Malachi, what happened at recess today?"

Malachi stopped dancing in place and paused to think.

"Ooooh...that..." he said, as if the encounter had happened weeks ago, "There was a boy on the playground who called me a monkey." I wanted to jump in and ask him what else had happened, but he continued, "But you know what, Mom? You have always said, 'Hurt people hurt people.' I figured he was just hurting. After he got in trouble and they sent him to the office, I did some research (yes, he said 'research,' just like a teacher's kid) and found out he lives in a pretty tough home. His dad says mean stuff to him all the time, and his older brother beats him up."

Here is a kid who was just called a name now doing his own research to figure out WHY!

"Mom, I've decided; I think he just needs a friend. I am going to make him my friend."

And I wanted to stand there and cry. How did this child develop this kind of empathy for others at such a young age, after all he had been through himself?

For your information, that child was one of the last people at our house a year later, as we loaded boxes onto the moving truck to move back to the West Side of our state.

You might wonder what this story has to do with systems.

This story's most obvious racially motivated element is where the other ten-year-old child called my son a monkey. The name-calling itself is not evidence of "systemic racism." However, I would argue that a lack of education in public schools has led to ignorance and misinformation for many White children about the history of race in this country. In most public schools, the only time any child learns about the experiences of Black people in America is the one- or two-week discussion about slavery and then, possibly (depending upon where children go to school), a Martin Luther King assembly.

Black people are reduced to two images—slave or superstar.

This is not the only place in the story that race is playing a role in systems. I know this from personal experience working in schools for almost thirty years. Still, for those of you who do not have that experience, there is a plethora of data about how Black boys with learning disabilities like ADD, ADHD, dysgraphia, and dyslexia are treated. On a national level, they are not provided with the support they need, even when they have the legal documentation to require that support. Many Black and Brown parents are not aware of how and when to acquire a 504 Plan to support the accommodations their children need, which means they do not often receive that support and then have no legal grounds to demand it. Even when we do, you now see the difficulty we have in getting their needs met.

Maybe there were other White children in my son's classroom who were also not flourishing, but that is not what I witnessed the few times I visited. That experience with his teacher in a small-town school north of Spokane would be repeated in another school much closer to our current home. In fact, Malachi would experience several dehumanizing encounters over his K-12 experience. It is a wonder he graduated on time. The even greater mystery is why he is now working towards becoming a teacher himself.

Another element of "systems" in this story relates to housing. Although that community north of Spokane was not designated "Whites only," it remains that way de facto. Many Black and Brown people, for generations, have been forced to purchase homes only in particular neighborhoods because that is what redlining allowed. Although by the time we moved to Spokane, redlining (the practice of banks only offering loans to Black people in particular neighborhoods) was no longer allowed, the practice had already established expectations for people. The message was clear to those who lived in Spokane that Black and Brown people were not welcome outside of certain neighborhoods, so they did not even attempt to move into new places. We were outsiders and did not know any different. We moved wherever we could find a home, without considering whether or not we would be welcome there.

The next element of "systems" in this story relates to policy and practice established in school buildings to address bullying and racially motivated hate speech. Far too many spaces—businesses and schools alike—are homogeneous and have only considered ways to respond to hate speech or actions that refer to religion or gender. When there are no Black or Asian or Latinx or Native students in your midst, it is easy to not think about a time when they may be in your presence, when you may have to think about different ways to support them and protect them from harm.

Even my son knew at ten years old that suspending another child for calling him a name was not an effective way to change his behavior or address the harm that had been done. Punishment is one thing. Accountability and restoration or reconciliation are completely different. Our collective healing will require the latter, but we have not embedded attitudes of restoration and reconciliation into our systemic practices. We remain a nation bent on punishment, which shows up in the numbers of students we suspend and expel from schools, as well as the numbers of people we incarcerate as a nation (the largest numbers per capita of any first-world country).

The last element of "systems" in this story is the lack of authentic relationships between those in authority and people of color. Malachi's first teacher only called when she had terrible news. She did not do the work of building a relationship with me and, in fact, broke the promise she made to me over the phone and then punished my son. The principal never did check in on us after "the incident" to see if things were going well for our son.

Although Malachi had a great relationship with his teacher (especially because he loved to talk about sports), that teacher never reached out to talk about the incident, either. What if we were not the people we are? What if we had not taught our child about empathy and modeled restorative practices in our home? That situation could have turned out very differently.

This story may be primarily about systems as they pertain to education, but I want you to consider parallel stories in your arena, whatever that is. For example, when have you seen a colleague who is raced as Black or Brown or Native experience treatment very differently from you—either invisiblized or targeted for behavior you have either demonstrated yourself or seen in other White colleagues? When have you seen people of color in your sphere punished more harshly for mistakes? In contrast, where have either you or another White colleague been severely punished for an action taken towards a Black or Brown colleague, instead of having the opportunity to apologize and make amends?

On a larger scale, there are systems at play around you every day that were established and are still influenced by stories of race that often privilege some and disenfranchise others. I have already mentioned "redlining" as one. If you are not familiar with that practice, I challenge you to do some research. I challenge you to learn about the redlining practices in your city or your state. The origins of these practices are shortly after World War II, when the men came home from war, and White men received low-interest loans for new homes, put towards college tuition, open a small business, or start a farm. The Black and Native men who had served the country in the same war were barred from access to those funds, which meant White men and their families could begin building wealth and accessing professional opportunities that were not available to people of color until many years later. This has implications for the United States in 2021 because some families have been able to live in communities with strong schools and quality food access for generations, while others have been forced to live in food deserts with some of the most poorly resourced schools. We may not be able to go back and change those realities, but what could be done in your communities to repair the harm those decisions, made over seventy years ago, have done to Black and Brown and Native people?

Of course, there were the practices to which we were all exposed in our American History classes—chattel slavery and, later, Jim Crow, the segregation of schools and businesses and bathrooms and religious institutions. Most people are also now aware of the internment of Japanese families during the war, along with the stripping of possessions and businesses. And then there are the countless broken treaties between the United States government and the Native people or the forced removal of Native children from their homes (up until the late 1970s, in some places) to attend boarding schools, where their heads were shaved, their languages forbidden, and their cultures stripped away by forced assimilation to the "ways of the White man."

For my White friends reading, there are two responses to these truths that are not useful:

1. Do not allow yourself to fall into the shame, blame, and guilt trap. You did not personally cause these things to happen. Shame, blame, and guilt will paralyze you, and they cause you to focus on yourself and not on the reality at hand. Snap out of those emotions and back into, "What can I do to make things better now?"

2. Do not allow yourself to fall into the trap of believing that because you did not personally own slaves and your family did not personally force Native peoples into boarding schools, your hands are clean. We are all either part of the problem or part of the solution.

Take time to learn about the system in which you have the greatest influence and commit to do at least something small to interrupt ONE practice that harms the Black, Brown or Native people affected by that system. Talk to your boss. Write a letter to a lawmaker. Join an advocacy group. Donate to an advocacy group that is already doing the work to make systemic change.

For the people reading who are raced as non-White, first realize that your mere presence is, in itself, an act of resistance. Continue to show up in your workplace. Speak up when you have the energy to do so. Engage in conversations and be willing to call out actions and statements that are harmful to you or to those around you. Find allies you can trust to go to when you do not have the energy to speak when the circumstances of life are too heavy to do more than just be present.

Finally, I would encourage you to create communities—virtually or in person—where you can have conversations about these issues, where you can share new learning, where you can talk about opportunities for change, for new practices, new legislation, new ways of doing business. There is enough work for all of us. No one person can do the work necessary to change systems in this country to allow for us all to flourish. We need to link arms, to be the bridges, when necessary, to connect decision-makers to new ways of looking at a problem, to new ways of mending broken fences. We cannot repair all of the harm at once, but if we can each, one step at a time, do something, and join forces whenever possible, a new season is possible.

# MOVING FORWARD FOR MYSELF

In an earlier chapter, I shared the story of how I started running after I ended my "career" as a basketball player. I talked about the training I had to do to prepare myself for that first half-marathon, and then I mentioned that I registered quarterly for different races after that just to force myself to stay running, to stay in shape.

Just before the pandemic, I was invited to join a Ragnar team that would run in July. The Ragnar is a nearly 200-mile relay race. Each team can have up to twelve members. The race is completed over days and involves vans in which runners sleep and rest when it is not their leg of the race. I could not have imagined being involved in a Ragnar five years ago, but I decided this would be a great way to keep myself motivated and force me to extend my regular workouts.

I began to train in February to be able to run two eight-mile non-stop runs in a day by the end of May, each leg at under nine minutes per mile. When the pandemic hit, knowing I would be running in the race in July gave me something to work on in my free time. I was very disciplined about running four to five times per week. My times were getting faster. I was able to run longer distances at a time. Well, that was true for the first two months. By the end of May, my shins and my Achilles were hurting. At forty-eight years old, my body was not liking the regular pounding on concrete. Until the pandemic, my body had become accustomed to running three days on a treadmill at the gym and only two days on concrete. Five days was just too much.

And then we learned the Ragnar was going to be canceled due to COVID 19. It almost felt like God was giving me a break. Phew! Now I did not have to feel bad about not being able to run so much in a week. There was nothing I had to be prepared for. It is one thing to let myself down. It is a whole different thing when a team is counting on you.

I set a new goal. By my birthday in June, I wanted to be able to run 3.1 miles (a 5K) in under twenty-seven minutes. That was a good compromise that would continue to stretch me but not destroy my legs. On June 3rd, I ran that 5K in twenty-six minutes and three seconds. I was really proud of my accomplishment.

I set a new goal—by the end of summer, I wanted to be able to run one mile in under eight minutes. I could already tell in June that COVID 19 was not letting up. I suspected we were not going to be able to head back inside to the gym anytime soon, so I needed to create a goal that would push me but would not do damage to my body.

I trained and timed myself at regular intervals. By the end of July, I had run one mile in eight minutes and five seconds. I was getting so close already. My goal was in sight!

I began to share my goal with others. I told all of my students—adults and children—about it. I told them I wanted to accomplish this goal by the end of the summer. One of my dearest friends, Fernell Miller, happens to be a physical education teacher. She offered to time my run to make the experience "official." We chose Labor Day.

I invited several friends to attend (masked, of course). The mother of one of my students asked if her soon-to-be sixth-grade daughter could join me. She had been in track at her elementary school.

I was excited to have one of my regular students running with me. This was going to be a fantastic experience!

On the day of the race, the wind was blowing hard from the east side of the field. I got to the track early to stretch and get myself mentally ready. I was worried about the wind. For one-quarter of the track, we would be running into the wind. That was not an exciting proposition at all. Suddenly, I was nervous. I had already timed myself once at just under eight minutes, but what if I was really slow today? In front of all these friends? What if I missed the mark? What if I did not meet my goal?

I had brought my iPad and tripod to film the entire proceeding. I planned to open on Facebook LIVE to allow others to join us who could not attend in person. Several friends showed up, including a young man from our youth group who had helped me train over the years. Two former colleagues showed up. My mentee showed up. My friend, the PE teacher, showed up, stopwatch in hand.

We opened with brief introductions on Facebook LIVE. Then we proceeded to the starting line. The sixth-grade student's five-year-old sister decided she wanted to run as well. Why not? The more, the merrier! We were only running one mile. She could do that, even if it took her a while.

Fernell blew her PE teacher whistle to start us. The student and her sister took off. Fast. One of my greatest strengths is pacing. I start at a decent pace, but I save my fastest running for the last one hundred yards or so. I figured the girls would tire out quickly. They had started much too fast. They were soon twenty yards ahead of me. I continued my usual pace, convinced the girls would slow down by the end of the first lap. The youngest slowed down, but the sixth-grader kept a consistent, fast pace. OMG! This kid... There was NO WAY I was going to keep up with her, but I also was not about to look stupid and let her lap me. I kicked it into a higher gear. I was determined not to let her get more than fifty yards ahead of me at any point.

I was convinced I was going to die. My lungs felt like they were going to explode. The wind on the East side of the field did not subside. I was convinced after my third lap that running into the wind alone was going to slow me down to the point that I would not reach my goal. I did my best to keep my student in sight. My lungs and legs were on fire in that last lap. Part of me just wanted to quit, to pretend I had a cramp and just pull off to the side. Another part of me was too proud to quit. I had told too many people I was going to do this race. I was determined to finish.

My student sprinted the last one hundred yards, and I ran as fast as I could behind her. I was not going to let myself get so far behind that I looked silly. Meanwhile, my friends were cheering us on from the sidelines, reminding us to pick up our knees and keep our eyes up and straight ahead. I could finally see the end in sight. I was not trained as a runner, but I remembered hearing from a state-champion sprinter years prior was, "Run through the finish line, not to the finish line."

Too many great, naturally fast runners slow down in the last few yards because they feel the end coming instead of imagining themselves beyond the finish line. Focusing beyond the finish line often shaves seconds off runners' times. I pictured myself running through the line and gave that last few yards my best, even though it felt like my entire body was going to explode.

"Seven minutes, twenty seconds, Erin! You killed your goal!"

What?! Had I heard her correctly? "Seven-twenty? How is that possible?"

She had the timer in her hand. The evidence was there.

On Labor Day of 2020, I ran a mile in seven minutes and twenty seconds.

However, just a month and a half later, I began to feel an incredible pain down the side of my shin, so I took a break from running. I had severe shin splints in college, and I could feel those coming on. I could not afford to do lasting damage to my body. I am too old at this point to heal quickly or completely. So I decided to take a month off, just to walk, instead of running.

Even after a month of walking, I continued to have severe pain near my shin. I already do not like going to the doctor, but I was not excited to go to the doctor during a pandemic. The pain was so great, though, I needed to know if there was damage that would require therapy or, even, surgery. I imagined the worst.

The doctor took a look and could not see anything, but he wanted to check for a microfracture, so he sent me to radiology for x-rays. The technician took photos of my lower leg from every possible angle, and then I had to wait, anxiously, alone, in the waiting room for the results. I imagined a stress fracture or a small break. I was imagining having to wear a boot. I was so sure that I had dug through my daughter's closet to see if her boot was still there from an old ankle injury. Before heading to the doctor, I put the boot out in my office to be ready, just in case.

The doctor could find no breaks—small or large—in my bones. However, he suspected I had a ligament that was twisted somehow. He recommended that I ice and heat alternately, and he suggested I just walk for the next month to allow whatever had caused the damage to heal fully.

I walked through December and then January. At the end of January, I attempted to run a 5K. I did not need to run quickly, but I thought I should be able to at least sustain the run. My body was screaming halfway through the first mile, "Erin, why are you out here!" I had to take a break and walk the second mile. I tried to run the third mile. Halfway through that, I just knew I was going to die, and my Achilles were hurting. Ok. Just stop, Erin. Don't try to overdo it.

I know now that I need to work my way back to 5K status. I know now that I may never run a mile in under eight minutes again, and I am ok with that. I just need to run. Running fast is not the point. The point is to continue to run. Who cares what my times are? Who am I comparing myself to? The only person that matters at this moment is me.

You are on a similar journey as you develop an equity mindset.

You are on a kick now, determined to strengthen your equity skills. You can read the whole book in one sitting, but that is like me trying to run the distance of a marathon in my first training session. There is no way to take in and effectively use everything in this book in one sitting. I would recommend going back and reading different pieces to see what new learning you get out of a story or a strategy.

You will have more or less motivation, more or less time to devote to learning about racial equity at different times in this process. Listen to your body. You will never "arrive" at ending racism on your own, so do not try. There are no books or podcasts you can listen to become the "expert." What you can commit to, though, is doing something four to five days per week, just like you would if you were training for a race.

You will encounter others who think you are doing too much. No one gets to decide what "too much" is but you. You may encounter others who are reading a book and taking a class and meeting in a community group, and marching in every protest, and you may wonder if you are doing enough. Once again, only you can decide when you are doing "enough." The work of equity is not a game, nor is it helpful to compare what you are doing or have done to anyone else. We are each on a journey. We are each going to go at our own pace. As long as you do not quit, you are on the right path.

I want to add that "the work" is not reading this book, listening to podcasts, or even attending rallies or marching in protest. Those things are good, but what will move the needle in this country is disrupting damaging attitudes, behaviors, and practices, building strong relationships between communities currently at odds, and influencing systems and organizations. You will know this work is taking root and having an effect when you witness bigotry in some form and step in to say or do something in everyday spaces like the grocery store. You will know you are on the right track when you read a document from work or see something on your school, business, or church website that reinforces dangerous narratives or proposes work that could harm, and you choose to say something to make the necessary changes. You will know you have gotten stronger when your family member says something at a holiday dinner and, instead of ignoring them, you say, "Hey! What you said right there is incorrect, and it is actually harmful. Can I share a different and more accurate perspective?"

Please remember to practice gratitude every day to establish the mindset that sets you up to do hard work. Practice "brave spaces" in every context—from home to work to community. Practice "grounding-in" before every hard conversation you have. Do the things that were introduced to you at the beginning of this book.

Doing the work of racial equity, committing to racial healing does not have an "end." You will never arrive "at" racial healing or equity. But, as long as you are doing something every day to learn, as long as you are challenging yourself to grow and stepping in to have conversations with your peers, colleagues, and family members about racial healing, you are moving in the right direction. I do this work for a living, and I continue to learn and grow. I challenge myself to listen to new voices and read new books as they come out. I challenge myself to be more patient with family members and Facebook "friends" as they demonstrate ignorance or obstinance on issues of race. Keep track of the encounters you have had online and in-person that have gone well. Let the successes motivate you to continue the process.

I want to encourage you to think about who is holding you accountable for this work. Who can you tell about the work? Who can you tell that you are on this journey that can ask you questions on occasion? Who will you allow to "call you in" when they see you silent or see you show up in ways that either perpetuate dangerous racial narratives or oppressive systems?

Again, you cannot do this work on your own. The work is too

hard, and you, alone, are not enough. For this nation to fully embrace an "US" mentality, it will take all of us to link arms and do the work. This is a journey we are all on. Whether you sprint or walk or run or crawl, do something. Be a bridge in every space in which you find yourself. Commit to building bridges in your community. Be a key element of healing US.

# PUSHING THOSE OUTSIDE MYSELF

W hat now?

What is your role in "healing US" now that you have done all this reading, and you have unpacked your story and "theirs" and ours? What can you do in your little classroom or office or neighborhood?

Healing US is a big lift that might feel overwhelming after all you have seen, heard, and read.

I have used a lot of sports metaphors and analogies. It is time for me to use another subject close to my heart to describe how I would recommend each of us move forward.

My parents met playing in a marching band in college. I learned recently that my father, who had been my math teacher, was also certified as a band instructor. My father plays trumpet. My mother played clarinet and piano. Music is an important part of the lives of everyone in our immediate and extended families. My cousins all played instruments, and they all sang in a touring choir my aunt directed.

Music was an expectation. Although I was an adopted kid, I tell myself the story that my biological father must have been a musician, because music of all kinds—playing instruments, reading music, singing harmony—all came naturally to me from the time I was little.

I picked up the recorder in fourth grade like every other student in my school, but my dad's partner teacher had various wooden recorders he played semi-professionally. Listening to him play interested me in playing more than the cheap plastic recorder we all received in music class.

I would transition from the wood recorder to a flute in fifth grade. I really wanted to play the drums or the saxophone. I thought those instruments were cool, but girls in the 1970s and 1980s were expected to play woodwind instruments. Mom had played clarinet in the band and understood woodwind instruments and reading music, so she was able to help me get started on the flute. Like most other things in my life, I devoted time beyond what was asked of me to become the best I could be. By the sixth grade, I had put in so many hours of practice that I was invited to play with the high school band. To participate alongside so many other instruments, with students who had such great skill, was both intimidating and wonderful.

I remember the first time someone was selected to do a solo. Oooh! I wanted to be that person someday. I wanted to be the star.

Over my many years in band, I was assigned my fair share of solos on the flute and clarinet. As much as I loved those opportunities, I also realized the pressure of being the one in the spotlight was not always fun. If I did everything perfectly, the experience was exhilarating. If I made a mistake, I would beat myself up for days, even if no one else heard it. It was actually kind of nice to be in the background providing harmony support to a soloist. My efforts were still appreciated. I got to be part of the group creating something beautiful.

One of the challenges inherent to this work is that we think we have to be the stars to make change. We have been told the ones who are up front doing all the talking are the ones who have the most value. The reality is that sometimes you can make the most significant changes from the background by supporting others.

When I got into teaching decades ago, I figured I would be like my dad—forty years in the classroom. I had zero intention of ever becoming an administrator. However, I took on a variety of leadership roles with the intention of using my position as a classroom teacher to move the system. Even as a substitute teacher, I coached teams. I attended every staff meeting. I asked questions. I critiqued the way things were done when I had alternative solutions. I stayed after school and worked with whatever team I was signed to help plan events and cross-curricular lessons. I volunteered to tutor students, especially Black girls, who were behind and needed additional support and mentoring.

In my first full-time teaching job, I volunteered to serve as our school improvement team leader. I had responsibility for writing agendas and facilitating meetings. I was also instrumental in helping our team look closely at which student groups we were serving well and which we were not. I attended trainings and learned more effective strategies for meeting the needs of my English Language Learners and those who were struggling to develop strong literacy skills. I was given opportunities to provide training to school staff.

I never had any intention of becoming an administrator. In fact, the many times principals would ask when I would get my admin credential, I said every time, "never!"

I even balked at the idea of applying for the instructional coach position at Rogers High School, fearing that I would end up not being around students, which is what I loved. Once I was offered the job, I asked if I could continue to work in a classroom at least once a day. I knew that I needed to keep my hand in the very thing I was hired to support other teachers to do. I ended up co-teaching a diversity class and then taking on a college-access class called AVID, in which I supported first-generation college students to have the experiences and develop the skills they needed to be ready for college.

At the end of my first year at Rogers High School, I saw the need for students to have dress clothes to wear for job interviews. So I created a clothing closet from which students (and eventually their families) could select clothes for interviews or after their family had experienced an eviction or house fire (both happened to students while I was there). I also offered to take on the Martin Luther King Jr. Day festivities, which my students facilitated for the two years I was there. My students got to learn a great deal about this American hero, and they were exposed to local leaders who gave short speeches at our events or shared their stories in my classroom.

I met a Black woman just a few years younger than me at a community event in Spokane. She and I came up with the idea to host a gathering for girls of color every Friday morning at the school. I brought pastries, and we invited different community members to join us once a month to share their stories and talk about life lessons. Our group started with just a couple of girls and blossomed into a classroom full of girls who continued to meet even after I took a job at the State Superintendent's Office.

Whether you are a classroom teacher or a Paraeducator or work in the lunchroom, there are ways you can make a difference, be a bridge, build a bridge for a young person who just needs a champion. Sometimes we talk about solutions as if they have to be large and affect a whole community. Sometimes, that small thing you do will blossom into something greater over time, as more people see value in the activity and link arms with you.

During my first year as the Assistant State Superintendent, I had a vision. As much as I was intentional about getting out into the community and not just staying in our offices in the state capitol, I also believed we as an agency needed to hear from members of the public whose voices were not often invited into that space. In 2009, I started a group I called "The Dream Team." I invited classroom teachers, administrators, and community-based organizations and activists to join me once a quarter for networking opportunities and then to provide input on the needs of communities of color as they saw them. I knew I could not possibly know all that I needed to know about the needs of students and communities around the state. I also knew there was not another space where like-minded groups seeking out the healing of communities of color could connect and leverage resources and opportunities for the greater good.

I am still friends with many of the people who participated in that project. What we did in those rooms together—organically sharing and dreaming and writing policy and critiquing programs—was powerful and life-changing for me as a state leader. I remembered what I learned as a flutist in the band in high school. As fun as it was to be the star, to have the title "Assistant State Superintendent," it was much more rewarding to watch an entire room full of equally passionate equity warriors descend on our offices once a quarter to make recommendations and connections that would affect Black and Brown students across the state for years to come.

After almost four years at the State Superintendent's Office, I knew that I needed to get back closer to teaching and students. I took a job as the Director of Equity for one of the largest districts in the state. In that role, I was responsible for programming in thirteen different buildings, from middle school through high school. I loved the opportunities to get into various facilities to work with administrators, teachers, and students. It was the best of all possible circumstances for my gifts and passions.

In my last year as an administrator, each of us at the district was given an assignment. One of our lowest-performing schools wanted to try an experiment. At the beginning of a new calendar year, just before the second semester began, the principal sent out a list of all seniors who were just one or two credits shy of on-time graduation. Those of us who were willing and able were assigned to sit with each of the students on our list. We read carefully through each one's transcript to see if there was a credit someone had missed, a failing grade a student could make up—anything that could get this student on track to graduate.

At first, the idea did not make sense. Why couldn't the counselors in the building do this work? Why were we, district administrators, not connected to students in this building taking on this task?

Well, the counselors had over 1,000 other students to tend to. They realized over time that some students had not graduated in the past because the counselors were overwhelmed and unable to ensure every student was registering and completing the coursework necessary to graduate on time. After a deep dive into transcripts, they had a theory that if they could get support, even just for a few weeks, they could increase their graduation rates significantly.

I chose to participate in the process. I got to know some students I had only seen in the hallways. I was able to talk them through their transcripts, which allowed them to see what they had already accomplished and to recognize how close they were to the end. Those encounters allowed me to help students frame the next steps. In the end, not only did we make sure they had the necessary coursework to graduate, but we were also able to get some of them thinking about attending a community college or technical school. What began as an annoyance developed into a powerful experience for all involved.

When I think about where you are and how you can support others outside yourself to do the work of racial justice and racial equity, I think about this story. We did not look for students who were a dozen credits shy of graduation just a semester out. That would have been futile. Those students did not require a deep dive into their transcripts. Those students needed a much more significant intervention. Even that was going to require a tremendous shift of attitude, desire, and willingness to work in a different way and at a different pace. As a district administrator with little to no relationship, I would not be the best intervention for those students. However, we at the district office were just the right fit for the students who were so close, who could see the end but just needed a push. We were not the same faces they had seen for almost four years (and were tired of at that point). We could provide some fresh perspective.

I want to encourage you to think about your circles of influence. Who in your family, friend, colleague circle has asked questions about race on occasion, who has at least demonstrated some level of curiosity about the topic? Who do you notice posting things on social media that are questionable or naive but not malicious? Start there. Start by sharing a meme, article, or short video on your social media or via text or email (depending on their preferred form of communication). You could send off a test balloon and see if they engage at all on their own. Then, depending on their level of engagement, you could continue in a similar fashion, just once a week.

Although I am not a huge fan of book clubs that do not lead to action, a book club is a good introductory step for those who just need to dip a toe in the water of race and equity. If you choose to do a book club, my recommendation is that you take it slow. Do not ask people to read more than one chapter at a time. That will give them time to process before they have to engage. It is also a manageable amount of reading. The last thing you want is to overwhelm people before they have even gotten their bearings.

I want to encourage you to get intentional about how you use social media. You do not need to post something every day but set a goal for yourself to post something related to race and justice once a week. If you do not feel comfortable creating your own content yet, follow folks who have expertise in equity—Dr. Christopher Emdin, Dr. Bettina Love, Dr. Brenda Salter-MacNeil, Dr. Pedro Noguera, Dr. Gholdy Muhammad. They post quite frequently about issues related to equity. Repost their material. Ask people what they think. There is no need to respond to everyone's comments. Depending on your reach, you may not have the capacity to do so.

If you work in a school or a non-profit, host a movie night or encourage people to listen to a powerful podcast and then create space for a panel discussion or town hall (depending on your context). There is power in talking about a piece of media that everyone has experienced. During the conversation, the burden is not on individuals to share their own experiences if they do not want to. Instead, the focus can be on what people heard or saw. I know of organizations that host monthly events like this. Over time, community is developed, which creates space for more courageous and vulnerable conversations.

Where could you share your journey of learning? What spaces are you in that you can share why you began this journey of addressing racial equity? Often, people are just not sure how to start, and, particularly for White people, they wonder if they have any "right" to be engaged if they are the ones who should be involved in this work. There is an assumption that social justice or racial justice work is the work of Black and Brown and Native people, when, in reality, the only way this work has any hope of success is if we *all* are engaged.

14

OBSTACLES

The last year and a half (from the start of 2020 to the middle of 2021) have been a *struggle*—physically, emotionally, mentally.

We have all lost things, been forced to change things, and embrace new ways of being. Some of you have lost people. Some of you have lost jobs. Some of you have lost security and peace of mind. Eighteen months ago, I entered a season of my life I would come to learn is called perimenopause. For those who have never heard of that, it is a season in a woman's life before menopause, when her body feels all the things that will come with menopause— the hot flashes, the memory lapses, the exhaustion, the bloating— but ALSO experiences all that comes with being of child-bearing age.

I had *no idea* the other things were coming — the COVID-19 pandemic, the racial conflict, the loss of life (nine friends over twelve months), the most contentious Presidential election in my lifetime, and the conviction of Derek Chauvin for the murder of George Floyd. All I knew was that hot flashes and bloating were horrible, especially while on the road, which I was during the beginning months of perimenopause.

I went from daily travel across the state and nation to being stuck on a computer all day, every day. In the middle of a keynote speech on Zoom, suddenly, it felt as if a literal fire had been lit inside my body. No matter what I was wearing at the time, I wanted it off. My armpits sweat. My lower back sweat. I wanted to make faces at the intense discomfort, but the challenge of Zoom webinars is that your face is right there, the only thing on display for all watching to see. It took any energy I had not to let the audience know I felt like my body was ready to combust right in front of them.

March was just horrible. I do not think I got one whole night of sleep because intense sweats woke me up two or three times per night. And then July came, and my body reminded me, "Hey, friend, this is actually just the dress rehearsal for the real thing! The joke is on you. You are nowhere near close to being done with this."

Perimenopause was finally followed by official menopause—entering a new season of life, which lasted almost a year. Perimenopause was uncomfortable. Menopause *sucked*.

I am someone who is used to having lots of energy. There were days when it was all I could do to stay awake during the training I was delivering. As soon as I had a break, I would head to my bedroom to take a catnap. If I had time, I would stay asleep for two to three hours in the middle of the day.

I have spent a lifetime always cold, needing extra layers and blankets, but my body has been like a walking radiator for the last year. Like many during the pandemic, I learned to wear a sleeveless blouse and jewelry up top, the only thing visible to the camera. My bottom half was always shorts or a tennis skirt. It was all my body could handle. My insides would light on fire anywhere from two to three times every hour. In fact, I cannot be thankful enough for going through this process in the privacy of my own home and not on stages in front of hundreds or thousands of people. This was terrible in its own way. That would have been horrific.

Now that I am "on the other side," I can see the benefits of going through this process. There are many things I will no longer have to tolerate. Although having completed menopause means my "youth" is officially behind me (this body will not produce any more babies), I am also stepping into an era of eldership. There are things I have learned about life, mistakes I have made, challenges I have endured, and wisdom from that learning I now get to impart to the next generation.

I have passed from one season to another.

For many of you, conversations about race have been like the last eighteen months have felt for me. You witnessed reactions to the election of President Obama. You witnessed very public murders of Black men and women by police and watched, or maybe even joined marches in support of Black lives. You watched the election of President Trump, who made public statements about Mexican people and Black people and Muslims and immigrants, and the support for those statements (or the silence) of friends and family blew your mind. It made no sense. These were good people you had known your whole life. They were church-going. You had gone on missions trips with them to Mexico and Haiti. They were great parents and spouses. How could they support such damaging, stereotypical rhetoric about the Black and Brown people in our nation?

In 2017 and 2018, you watched friends and public figures criticize Colin Kaepernick for taking a knee during the playing of the National Anthem. You watched them on social media, heard them at family dinners as you watched NFL games talk about how unpatriotic and ungrateful people like Kaepernick were, "Oh, and he's no good anyway. They should just fire him."

And then he was let go and never rehired, and you watched as people across the country continued to critique his stand and then burn their Nike clothing when he was made the face of the "Just Do It" campaign. You witnessed YouTube videos and Facebook posts of people in your circle stating they would never purchase Nike again and claiming they would stop watching NFL games if the league continued to allow "those ingrates" to devalue the contributions of America's veterans.

You watched students in your school or your child's school or at the local college take a knee before games and heard the murmuring (and sometimes yelling) of other fans, demanding that coaches make students stand. And then there would be another shooting, another questionable encounter between police and a Black man, and there would be more marches and counter-marches.

Our body... US... the United States... felt like it was going to burn up from the inside out, just like my body had felt ready to explode. Book clubs sprang up across your community. Even in predominantly White towns, people were marching for Black lives, so it felt for a moment like progress was being made.

And the COVID-19 pandemic hit, and you began to see which communities were hit the hardest—Black, Latinx, Native—the very same communities that had always been pushed to the margins, the same communities that had always struggled for access to health-care and stable housing and quality education, and you heard people say things like, "Well, if they would just eat more healthy food" or "If they would just exercise more and take care of their bodies."

You realized the gift you had, being able to do work from home and be safe at home, as many in the margins remained on the front lines in jobs that put them and their families at risk day in and day out. You realized the gift that you and most of your friends had in your ability to teach from home. As hard as it was, you had decent internet service and access to all the necessary technology to support your family.

And then Ahmaud Arbery was killed, his murder filmed by friends of the murderers. You watched family and friends, again, respond in ways that were so surprising to you, "Well, if he had just stopped and answered their questions. If he had not gone into that abandoned home. If he had not fought back." And you realized the season we had been in before the pandemic was just our own "social perimenopause." As a nation, we were not in a "better place" yet.

And then we learned of the death of Breonna Taylor... and then George Floyd... The nation and then the world seemed to erupt in response: Black Lives Matter. Marches with responses from Antifa and Proud Boys escalated everything to the levels that more police were involved and, on occasion, the National Guard appeared.

All the while, you watched the nation walk through the most antagonistic, publicly contentious Presidential election in your lifetime. You watched a President and supporters call the results fraudulent and witnessed a refusal to concede. You heard of threats of violence by those who believed ballot boxes and electronic systems had been tampered with by those who wished to destroy democracy.

As 2021 began, and a new President was preparing to be inaugurated, you hoped for a fresh start, but then January 6, 2021 happened. Hundreds of people, many of whom were middle-class professionals, invaded the nation's capitol in protest of an election they claimed had been mismanaged.

After the March 16 spa shootings targeting Asian women, you learned there had been close to 4,000 anti-Asian racist incidents, mostly against women, in the year from March 2020 to March 2021.

What? How could you have not known this? Why wasn't this information more public? How have we become this as a nation? Was this really the US?

This. Was. US.

Watching these incidents unfold made you realize we were something different than you had imagined. You had been reading books and watching videos, and listening to podcasts. You knew some of your friends and colleagues had been doing the same. You were shocked at the colleague (or family member) you heard about who planned to attend the January 6 insurrection. You were shocked by the ways some of your friends and family showed up on social media.

I saw this among my friends and family members, and fellow church congregants. Talking about race is *hard*, y'all.

I teach about the difficulty of these conversations almost every day, and I still struggle with what to say and how to say it, what to do and how to ensure "it" happens.

You are going to struggle, too. There will be times your body breaks into a sweat at the mere thought of confronting a boss about something said in a meeting or a parent who does not understand why you keep posting "that race stuff" on Facebook.

We are collectively walking through a new season in our nation. Unlike my body that moves through biological processes on its own clock and over which I have ZERO control, we as the United States get to decide if this is our moment if we are willing to embrace the challenges that will lead to our healing. Our racial healing is not going to come just because it is time. Our healing will not happen by accident. Our healing requires each of us to engage, wherever we are, with whomever has been placed in our circle to influence.

There will be days, no matter how many books you read and classes you take, when your best words are going to land wrong on a family member or colleague who is just not ready for the conversation. You will need to go back the next day or week, or month and have the conversation again.

Do not give up.

There will be days when you will try something that has worked multiple times before. Suddenly, that statement, that tactic will fall flat. Do not let that failure cause you to not try the same thing again later with someone else.

Do not give up.

I pride myself on the ability to create the kinds of environments in which people, even those who are novices to this conversation, feel comfortable with the discomfort of difficult conversations. I have been doing training for schools and businesses and govern-

146

ment agencies, and non-profits for years. I do not claim to be the expert, and there are likely plenty of people who are better teachers and speakers than myself, but I think I am pretty good at what I do. For the most part, I can create spaces where people are brave and willing to engage in the difficult work of talking about race, of interrogating their stories.

Even so, there have been occasions when attendees have complained about any mention of race. For example, on one occasion, a White executive stood up in the middle of training and announced that he had never experienced White privilege (a thing I had not even mentioned yet) and then walked out of the training.

I learned not to talk about things like "White privilege," "microaggressions," or "racism" in the first session. Instead, I learned to draw people in, have people do some identity work first, connect to WHY conversations about race were so critical, and then introduce the "tough" stuff.

That was a successful tactic... until George Floyd was killed.

The new iteration of the #BlackLivesMatter movement that was initiated across the world in June 2020 also inspired a movement by the conservative right to critique any and all conversations about race as heretical, regardless of the tone of the conversation or the love with which a message was delivered. National evangelical Christian leaders, who had never seemed interested in a conversation about race before, created formal statements referencing Critical Race Theory (CRT) as the greatest threat to Christianity in modern history. CRT became a lightning rod for division within the church community, a flashpoint for liberals and conservatives.

Social media became the canvas on which "us" versus "them" played itself out daily. I watched my Black and Brown Christian friends post in support of Black Lives (not even with specific reference to the organization #BLM), and I watched White friends, who had sat in the same pews for years, post #AllLivesMatter and #BlueLivesMatter, along with an assortment of memes and articles describing the dangers of Marxism and "reverse racism," as if anyone who cared at all about conversations related to race and justice must necessarily be a Marxist and could not possibly be Christian. Suddenly, the focus of many conservatives was on #BLM being the reason for the downfall of the United States.

I knew that the foundations of my learning and instruction about race and justice were not formed by Critical Race Theory. What I know and teach about racial justice and equity was developed over time by personal experience, studying history, and working in the very systems in which I had seen and experienced incredible inequity. Have I learned from those who have been informed by Critical Race Theory? Sure, but that is not the foundation for the instruction I deliver on the subject.

As I watched greater, more intense division between friends and family I have known for decades, I decided maybe I could put my experiences and expertise to good use by offering a free course to people from my church. My husband is an elder. We talked about the possibility of taking the work I was doing with businesses and adapting it for a new audience. He offered to support me in teaching the class. He is a teacher as well, and he has done his own bridge-building around issues of race in his lifetime.

At the beginning of our first session, before we could even get through introductions, a woman unmuted herself and asked how we might have been "allowed" to do this training. She said the training in itself (which we had not yet begun) was heretical, and she could not believe our pastor was allowing it to happen. Then she disappeared from the call.

There was silence.

Fortunately, I was a middle school teacher for over a decade, and my husband is a ninth-grade English teacher. We are not easily deterred, so we continued to teach the course—four sessions—as well as manage a Facebook group in which people could interact between sessions.

The opening engagement and the ways people engaged on Facebook were more contentious than anything I had experienced in the formal trainings I delivered to government agencies, schools, or businesses.

I was not only going through physical menopause. This felt like spiritual menopause. It was disorienting. It was exhausting. It was painful, at times.

I knew there were extreme differences of opinion and perspective in my church because I was seeing them on Facebook almost daily in the ways people were responding to the news—their views on police, masks, protests, riots, when it was okay to disobey law, when it was not okay. As we neared the election primary, I watched people put up political posts that shocked me. No one talked politics in church, so, although I knew many leaned conservative, I had no idea until the pandemic, when people were "forced" to do all their communications virtually (and, therefore, publicly) the extent to which political conservatism was a norm among many of the White members of my church.

I decided not to post anything explicitly political (Democrat or Republican), although I am sure every post in which I talked about race and justice was perceived as political. I have found in the current climate in the United States, conversations about race are only allowable in Democrat spaces, and there is an assumption by many evangelicals that all "good Christians" must be Republican. So confusing to me!

I intentionally did not post anything about #BlackLivesMatter, either because I watched my friends' pages. Anytime the hashtag was used, strangers showed up to say ugly things to and about them, to call my friends Marxists and baby-killers and race-baiters.

As someone who does racial justice and racial reconciliation work, I knew that I could not allow myself to get sidetracked by conversations that would not promote healing. When friends asked, I would say I support "Black lives mattering" by helping schools and organizations better serve and resource Black people. I support "Black lives mattering" with my mere presence in the world by walking in my neighborhood and saying hello to people as they walk by me.

The Presidential Primary arrived, and with it, an even more clear divide between people around issues of race. I do not know that I have experienced greater spiritual and mental disorientation in my adult life than I experienced from the time of the Primary to the General election and then the two weeks that followed, as the race for President was officially certified.

I watched as people in my world argued on Facebook, as news came to me of things being said about me and my work by people I had known almost half my life. My body was burning from the inside out, but I also felt the singe of fire from outside me, from what I thought had been friendships.

Fortunately, during this season, I also became connected to others via Twitter who described similar experiences. These people were White, Black, and Asian. They were other people who described themselves as having faith similar to mine but feeling ostracized by the faith communities in which they had participated because of the ways that talk of race was vilified.

I learned to build community wherever I could find it. Much like physical menopause propelled my body into a new season of life, this last year has propelled me into new communities of people (primarily virtual, but not always) with whom I can commiserate and lament and laugh and celebrate.

I have walked with my friend Sheri probably thirty weekends over the last year. We walk and talk and plot to save the world and bring racial healing to our spaces of influence. I have invested in my friend Khurshida, as she cooks comfort food weekly to provide the community with access to healthy food and using additional proceeds to then feed people in homeless shelters or otherwise without access to food. I have met in Zoom rooms with students, parents, and educators at least once a week, who I now call my community. My dear friend, Ty, who I met through church, supports me as my assistant and makes sure I get on the right Zoom links and get breaks between events. Dr. Jen Self and Fernell Miller and I record a podcast weekly to share our thoughts on current events and how those are affected by White Supremacy Culture. I walk to my parents' house or drive there to say HI from a distance or, now that we are all vaccinated, sit in their living room and talk about... whatever. I text with my daughter, who lives in Seattle, and we share TikTok videos that make us laugh. Several friends who are educators in different spaces (even one from states) reach out to me each week to check in to see if there are ways they can support me.

And then there is my immediate family—my amazing husband, who has tackled teaching freshman English and History remotely and in-person, been a head football coach and taken over a church when the pastor left with little warning; and my two amazing young adult sons who remind me every day that, no matter what else is happening in the world, we raised some all-around unique humans, who are kind and loving and witty and silly, and who are equally passionate about being and building bridges of racial healing in their spheres of influence.

This work is not for the faint of heart, and it cannot be done on your own. If you do not yet have a community, create your own. The most beautiful outcome of the pandemic for me is not that I am now no longer suffering from menopause but that this virtual world has connected me to so many others eager and ready to be and build bridges of racial healing.

Who are your people? Where are you finding a community of others who are committed to being on this journey, others who are being burned by the fires of this moment, who are unsure of their next moves? How are you using social media to connect to people moving through this moment in similar ways? What news sources are you listening to get balanced reports about what is happening in your local community and across the nation? Who is holding you accountable for self-care?

15

# CONCLUSION

I struggled most with finding a story to tell to open this chapter. Tonight, we were all up, later than usual for us old ones. The four of us stood in the kitchen talking—my husband, my two sons, and I, after 11:00 PM on a Sunday night.

I was up because this manuscript was due to my editor tonight by midnight.

My husband was up because he and my oldest are addicted to talking about football. They were sitting at the dining room table talking about who could play quarterback next year (why that is important on this night, months from summer camp, I do not know).

My youngest asked how things were going upstairs. He also had his final paper due today for grad school. I shared that I felt pretty good about my other chapters but that I struggled hard with the conclusion.

My oldest son stopped what he was saying to my husband, stood up, and shouted from the other side of the room, "Mom, maybe you are having a hard time writing a conclusion, because there isn't one, because you have been working so hard on this problem, and it's so big, there is just not a conclusion yet."

He is not wrong.

I was hoping to end with a witty, thought-provoking story, but I am stuck, I think because there is both too much to say and not enough to say to get people to move in the "right direction."

I am out of words. You have them, all that I can muster at the moment.

I want to remind you that this work requires beginning with gratitude. I want you to continue to practice gratitude at every opportunity. We need to start every hard thing by recognizing how we have been blessed, remembering what we already have in our hands and who we have in our lives.

I want to remind you to push back against the idea of certain behaviors being "normal." The next time someone in your work-space posts "meeting norms" up on the wall or a PowerPoint slide, I want to encourage you to suggest "community agreements" as a way to invite in a more inclusive attitude about who "gets to" set the tone for meeting expectations. I want to encourage you to focus on creating brave and courageous spaces instead of safe (which I think is impossible). We have tiptoed around these issues for far too long, trying to make sure people feel comfortable. Look where we are as a nation. In the end, no one is safe. Our lack of courage in this arena is causing division.

What might it mean for people in your context to be their "best and bravest" selves? It is worth taking a meeting or two to have an in-depth conversation and then to revisit whatever decisions you make quarterly or semi-annually. The needs of your community may change over time based on new members joining your team or events that shake things up in some way. Always be willing to adapt and adjust.

Remember that "diversity" is just the beginning. Studying people's differences or knowing about them is just one step in the process. Multicultural potlucks and celebrations are lovely, but in themselves, they are not going to shift the culture of your work-space or create better outcomes for anyone. Please celebrate Dr.

Martin Luther King Jr's birthday and Juneteenth. Please recognize the wide variety of winter holidays in December and not just Christmas, but those things alone will not change your systems. If nothing else is happening to shift how people are being hired or supported, doing those superficial, celebratory things can feel like harm or disingenuous.

To get to racial equity requires that you begin with yourself, that you are constantly paying attention to how you move through the world—where you are experiencing barriers and where you are getting lots of support. Pay attention to the ways systems work for you or do not, for whatever reason. Pay attention to what events in the news or at work make you either angry or upset or sad. Do the self-work to figure out why.

Take the time to discover who is in your community that you do not know... yet. Who are the people that appear, on the surface, to be most unlike you? Decide to walk alongside some new people. Choose to show up in their spaces, not just once, but over and over and over. Witness how they are experiencing local and national news, how they are experiencing systems. Have conversations about what success and thriving might look like to them. Do not judge them if their responses are completely different from your own. I promise you will begin to recognize different ways you can show up to them to be a true ally and friend, and that will also help you as you return to your job and see ways you may be able to apply that learning to decisions and practices in that context.

Instead of starting your social justice organization or writing your policy initiative, find out which Black-, Brown- and Native-led organizations are already putting together political platforms. Volunteer to support those. Which Black, Brown, or Native people are running for office in your community? Find one with whom a policy initiative resonates and offer to support their campaign in some way—either monetarily or with the gift of time.

If you are someone in a position of power or are connected to someone with influence, insist on hearing direction from Black,

Brown, and Native people before making policy changes, writing your equity statement, or hiring that new Director of Equity. Make sure Black and Brown and Native people are not only at the table for important conversations and decisions; make sure they are heard, and their words are taken seriously and acted on somehow. Remember, if you are a White person, it is not your job to speak FOR Black and Brown and Native people. Whenever possible, it is your job to make space, to insist that others make space for them.

In those times when you want to quit, when it all feels overwhelming, when you feel like your little actions and voice do not matter, keep moving forward. Keep reading. Keep listening. Keep writing. Keep posting. Make sure you surround yourselves with others who are committed to the work so you can practice spurring one another on. It helps to have regular reminders that you are not alone on this journey. Also, remember that your journey and your racial healing and justice work will not look exactly like anyone else's. Your journey will be unique because you have your own unique set of experiences and circumstances.

Since I was nineteen years old, I have talked about myself as a bridge and a bridge-builder. It was apparent to me that I was physically designed as a bridge even at that young age. My life story has been written to help me bridge gaps—from one language to another, one culture to another, one country to another.

Another reality I have come to realize and vocalize more recently is this, "Bridges connect to places, but bridges also get walked on... and sometimes with heels."

Being a bridge is at the same time rewarding and painful.

Although I know I was uniquely made to be and build bridges for racial healing, I absolutely believe there are so many more of you out there with similar stories. Maybe you are not physically designed to BE a bridge, but I hope you can now see how you could be part of the design team for a bridge. Maybe you are an artist, and you can visualize and draw a bridge. Maybe your expertise is math, and you can be a member of the engineering team. Perhaps another one of you has access to the materials needed—wood, steel, brick—to actually make the design a reality. Maybe you own a trucking company, and you are now seeing ways you could transport people or ideas across the bridge after it is built.

There are enough bridges that need to be built—of all kinds—that we can use you and whatever skills and stories you bring to the table. The work of racial healing and justice in the United States is massive and will take an army of committed workers to get US to a place of healing. I feel honored to be on this team with you. This work is hard, but I have incredible hope. I am thankful to the thousands of people who have shown up at my trainings or my Facebook LIVE events over the years. I am so grateful to my parents, who really had no idea what they were getting into when they held that little caramel-skinned baby in the Children's Home Society nursery in 1971. They have given everything, invested so much money, time, and energy to help me become the best version of myself possible, and they continue to show up for me, for my family, for my friends.

Whether you are a talker or a quiet behind-the-scenes actor, there is something each one of you can do to move the work of racial equity and healing forward. We need the loud ones and the quiet ones, the writers and the dancers, the statisticians and the storytellers, the marchers, and the poets to get the work done required for healing US.

I know this is big work, and you cannot do it all on your own. I know this. I have seen you trying to understand it. But do not wait for an army to begin your own work. Instead, start with you and figure out how you can use what is in your hand and heart to connect to others.

Just start. And then do not stop.

I want to close my book with one more story, one which fills me with hope among many things and that I believe exemplifies the heart of my message and what we can feel when we commit to being and building bridges.

I met Jarod Higginbotham on a plane from Seattle to the small town of Yakima in Central Washington. It was January 19 of 2020. I remember the date because it was the day before the national celebration of Dr. Martin Luther King, Jr. I was scheduled to speak at an event for the city and was flying in the day before to stay with a dear friend.

In 2019 I flew so much I was often bumped to first class if I arrived at the airport early enough. On this particular flight, I was given my favorite seat—1A, right up front, where my very long legs would have room to stretch.

I sat down, and just minutes later, one of the tallest men I have ever met entered the plane, bent over to avoid banging his head on the doorway, and sat next to me in seat 1B.

I will never forget the giant smile on his face or his fabulous blue suede shoes. "Hey! My name is Jarod."

Jarod is 6'10". I am 6'. We are both giants for our genders.

Jarod and I grew up on opposite sides of the world—me in Europe, moving among international executives and political leaders from dozens of nations, him in a small town north of Yakima, where everyone looked and sounded like him. I travel the country speaking in front of educators and government agencies about racial equity. Jarod is a professional fisherman who sells fishing gear and speaks about fishing techniques at sportsmen shows.

Jarod and I talked every minute of the flight. We may have grown up in completely different environments, but we are both gentle, happy giants. We both embrace our height and love fun shoes (we talked a LOT about our love of fun shoes). We both love opportunities to meet new people and see every new connection as a potential friend.

We had someone take a photo of us as we waited to pick up our luggage in baggage claim. I posted the picture on Facebook and Instagram. Jarod found the photo and tagged himself. We began to follow one another on social media. I learned more about his children, and he learned more about my husband and children. Two weeks after we met, I learned by following his posts on Instagram that he would be presenting at a fishing conference in Puyallup, at the local fairgrounds past which I would be traveling on my way home from a keynote speech in Kent.

I happened to arrive late enough that the entrance fee was waived. I knew the name of Jarod's company and entered the exhibition hall looking for his booth. Jarod was not at the booth, but his colleagues let me know he was about to do an interview on the local fishing station, recorded live, from one of the other exhibition halls. I went searching for him and arrived just as he was beginning to speak.

He was already mid-sentence when I showed up at the back of the room. Although I couldn't stay for the entire interview, I stayed long enough for him to see me, to experience his brilliant smile again.

Jarod and I remain dear friends to this day. He lost his wife to cancer several years ago. I have watched him raise his children on his own. He and his young adult daughter joined my middle and high school "Becoming a Change Agent" virtual class as special guests shortly after the pandemic began. He shared with my mostly urban students about his life in rural Washington and his job as a fisherman. Jarod has watched me navigate issues of race and mourn the losses of eleven friends in the last year, and he reaches out regularly to check on me.

As soon as we can travel freely, Jarod has offered to host us all— my husband and our children. He—a man I have met in person once and seen only one other time—has offered to cook for us and host us. He sees me as a sister. I see him like a bigger, younger brother. We may not talk about race and issues of racial healing every time we communicate, but he gives me incredible hope for the future. If only we could all get curious about one another, especially from urban to rural, from White to Black, imagine what is possible?

Stay grateful for every encounter.

Stay curious about those around you.

Stay learning.

Don't be paralyzed by not having the exact right answer.

Keep moving and speaking and disrupting and investing.

Keep being and building the bridges we need to heal US.

Do you see me on the track? I am running in front of you, behind you, alongside you, reminding you when your lungs burn to keep going, reminding you to keep your eyes on the prize.

Run through the finish line, my friends! You've got this! We've got this!

# ABOUT THE AUTHOR

Erin Jones is a biracial, transracial adoptee, originally adopted from Minnesota but raised by her educator parents at the American School of The Hague in the Netherlands. She attended Bryn Mawr College and went on to earn her teaching certificate from Pacific Lutheran University. She has now been involved in and around schools for thirty years. She has taught in various environments, from predominantly Black to predominantly White to some of the most diverse communities in the nation.

Erin received an award as the Most Innovative Foreign Language Teacher in 2007, while teaching in Tacoma and was the Washington State Milken Educator of the Year in 2008, while teaching in Spokane. She received recognition at the White House in March of 2013 as a "Champion of Change" and was Washington State PTA's "Outstanding Educator" in 2015. She received recognition as a "Woman of Distinction" from the Seattle Storm in 2020. After serving as a classroom teacher and instructional coach, Erin worked as an executive for two State Superintendents.

Erin left the Office of Superintendent of Public Instruction in 2012 to work in college-access at the school district level. After five years in school district administration, Erin decided to run as a candidate for State Superintendent and was the first Black woman to run for any state office in Washington State, a race she lost by a mere 1%. Erin has three adult children: a daughter who graduated from Central Washington University and works for the Equity in Education Coalition, a son who graduated from Harvey Mudd

College and is in his last year of graduate school at USC and one who attends college and coaches high school football with her husband of twenty-seven years, James, who is a teacher and head football coach at Timberline High School in the North Thurston School District.

When the pandemic stopped schools and travel in March, Erin lost all her paid work, but she decided to take her skills and passion online. She offered eighty-three days of free teaching to both children and adults from mid-March to the end of June. Her choice to engage, especially as racial and political conflict erupted across the nation, created a platform for her to be more engaged as a speaker and trainer now than ever in her career. She has logged thousands of hours on Zoom delivering keynotes, doing school assemblies, and providing training to government agencies, nonprofits and schools, and she continues to facilitate free virtual gatherings for adults and children several days per week.

# THANK YOU

As one more thank you for reading my book and committing to making a difference in your sphere. I wanted to offer you a few free gifts. First, you will find links to some of my speeches and webinars so that you can continue your journey. Second you will see my contact information so that you can get in touch with me and watch out for more content and free resources as they become available.

I'm honored to be on this journey of healing US alongside you and look forward to seeing how you and I Be and Build bridges together.

~Erin

## Sample TEDx Talks
"Passion for Change" – https://youtu.be/HQ7xY60a6z4 "Be A Bridge" at https://youtu.be/hFc9axy2ktQ.

## Sample Podcasts/Webinars
https://www.characterstrong.com/webinar/43/developing-an-equity-lens

https://podcasts.apple.com/us/podcast/the-characterstrong-podcast/id1454582540?i=1000495242954

**Contact**
Email: erin@erinjonesdreams.com (for assistant: ty@erinjones-dreams.com)
Facebook: Erin Jones 2016
Instagram: erinin2016
Twitter: @erinjonesin2016
LinkedIn: http://linkedin.com/in/erin-jones-8a24a814